I WAS C

I WAS CICERO

ELYESA BAZNA

in collaboration with

HANS NOGLY

TRANSLATED BY ERIC MOSBACHER

HARPER & ROW, PUBLISHERS

New York and Evanston

FIRST EDITION

M—M

LIBRARY OF CONGRESS CATALOG CARD NUMBER: 62–20105

How This Book Came to Be Written

He told me on the telephone in not very good English that his name was Elyesa Bazna, that he was a business man from Istanbul, and that he was no other than Cicero, the great spy of the Second World War. We arranged to meet at the Vier Jahreszeiten Hotel in Munich, and when we did so I began by mistrusting him completely.

When I walked into the hotel a short, bald, thickset, elderly man with a wistful look in his eyes came forward to meet me. The wistfulness had nothing to do with me; his eyes had been lingering on a pretty girl who had just walked out.

The first thing he said to me—this time in French—was: "What a lot of pretty girls there are in Munich."

We had some desultory conversation before coming to the point. He mentioned that he liked sitting in hotels and watching people. Then I asked him if he were really Cicero.

He had been sitting relaxed in his chair, but at this he drew himself up. His dark eyes flashed, and he looked at me piercingly; he was indignant at doubt being cast on his word. His eyes, then and later, were the only thing about him that suggested that here was a man capable of being dangerous, crafty, and of shrinking at nothing.

He laid a green exercise-book on the table, an ordinary, child's exercise-book. It was filled with ornate handwriting.

"This is my life-story," he announced challengingly and with an air of finality, as if to forestall the scepticism that he expected of me.

I remarked that it was well known that men never lied or embellished the truth so much as when they committed their own life-stories to paper. He gave me a piercing, savage look. Then a sudden change came over his face, and he grinned broadly. My interlocutor was now a quick-witted Levantine interested only in the prospect of a deal, no matter whether it was in carpets, lap-dogs, or life-stories. Then he laughed outright, as if he were telling me an excellent joke.

"You're perfectly right," he said, chortling with pleasure. "You're perfectly right, of course. In that notebook I have made myself out to be a great hero and an even greater patriot." He winked one eye. "I have a mighty fine opinion of myself. Everyone has."

After that he put his cards on the table and made no attempt to hide anything from me. He turned out to be full of vanity, secret fears, and extravagant yearnings for smart and expensive living. With the help of the green exercise-book (in which he indeed flattered himself greatly) and his irrepressible outbursts of candour, the true picture of his life and adventures gradually emerged.

I asked him why, after hiding away for so long, he had suddenly decided to sell his life-story.

"I need the money," he replied. "I want to take legal action against the Federal German Government. Germany owes me money. I was grossly cheated by the German Reich. I want compensation from the Federal Government for the money the Germans cheated me out of when I spied for them."

(If he really embarks on legal action to recover damages for the forged British bank-notes with which his war-time espionage services to the Germans were rewarded, I have no doubt that the case will drag on to all eternity, for one of his qualities of which there can be no possible doubt is his pertinacity. But that part of the story lies in the future.)

There were some gaps in his memory. After all, seventeen years had passed since his great adventure. But he was always able to point out where inquiries could most usefully be initiated in order to fill them in. Two reporters—Herr Hans Schwarz, of Munich, and Mr. G. Thomas Beyl, of Hollywood—spent months following up all the details of the story, and a third, Herr Herbert Kaufhold, of Munich, checked points about which Bazna could no longer be positive because of the lapse of time. He and I are greatly indebted to these three gentlemen.

The thing that finally required corroboration was the genuineness of this at first sight improbable individual's claim to have been Cicero. For this purpose we applied to Herr L. C. Moyzisch, now resident at Innsbruck, who was Cicero's contact man with the Germans, and a confrontation was duly arranged. It was a strange, cool, and formal meeting. The two principal partners in this extraordinary business found that they had little to say to each other. But Herr Moyzisch supplied the missing link in the chain. He confirmed that Elyesa Bazna had indeed been the world-famous Cicero.

HANS NOGLY

Munich
February, 1962

Dramatis Personae

Sir Hughe Knatchbull-Hugessen
: British Ambassador in Ankara

Lady Knatchbull-Hugessen
: The British Ambassador's wife

Douglas Busk
: First Secretary at the British Embassy in Ankara

Franz Von Papen
: German Ambassador in Ankara

Albert Jenke
: First Secretary at the German Embassy in Ankara

Frau Jenke
: Wife of Herr Jenke and sister of Ribbentrop

L. C. Moyzisch
: Attaché at the German Embassy in Ankara

Elyesa Bazna
: Called "Cicero"—an Albanian *kavass*, valet to the British Ambassador

Cornelia Kapp
: Assistant Secretary to Herr Moyzisch and an agent of the American secret service

Mara
: Nursemaid to Mr. and Mrs. Busk's child

Esra
: A distant cousin of Cicero's

Aika
: A friend of Cicero's

Mustafa
Zeki
Manoli
: Servants at the British Embassy

A group of photographs will be found following page 68.

I WAS CICERO

CHAPTER 1

THE DAILY EXPRESS, January 30, 1950: *"In a Belgian news-paper an astonishing story is being published. It tells how in 1943 the Germans obtained vitally important Allied war secrets by paying £300,000 in sterling to the valet of the British Ambassador in Turkey, Sir Hughe Knatchbull-Hugessen. In this way, it is said, they learned of the Moscow and Casablanca conference decisions, details of the bomber offensives, and plans for the final invasion of Europe. They also obtained the key to the British diplomatic code."*

Yes, they did. And the man who sold this information to them was I, Elyesa Bazna.

The British tried to play my activities down, but they could not deny them.

HANSARD 478, 2023–4 (October 18, 1950): MR. SHEPHERD *asked the Secretary of State for Foreign Affairs in view of the fact that top secrets, including Operation Overlord,* were stolen from our Embassy in Turkey and transmitted*

---

* The code name for the Second Front.

1

to the Germans, whether an inquiry has taken place; what has been the result; and what instructions have been issued to prevent a repetition.

MR. BEVIN: *No such documents were actually stolen from His Majesty's Embassy during the war. But an inquiry into the occurrences to which the hon. member refers reveals that the Ambassador's valet succeeded in photographing a number of highly secret documents in the Embassy and selling the films to the Germans. He would not have been able to do this if the Ambassador had conformed to the regulations governing the custody of secret documents. New instructions have since been given to all concerned and other measures have been taken to prevent such leakages occurring again.*

MR. SHEPHERD: *Is it not a fact that the statement published in the book* in which this question arose caused a good deal of public anxiety; and if it was the case that the Overlord plans were not in fact stolen, why did not the Foreign Office issue a denial of the statement?*

MR. BEVIN: *The actual document was not stolen. I admitted that a photograph was taken, which is the same thing.*

Of course it was the same thing, and because of it there was a time when bank-notes to the value of £300,000 were carefully laid out under the carpet of my room in the servants' quarters of the British Embassy in Ankara. When I trod on them, in the guise of a faithful servant of the British Ambassador, Sir Hughe Knatchbull-Hugessen, I gloated.

---

* *Operation Cicero* by L. C. Moyzisch, the account of this affair from the German point of view (Coward-McCann, New York, 1951).

I had come a long way to collect that £300,000. My father, Hafiz Yazar, a Muslim religious teacher and the owner of two pieces of land, was a devout, God-fearing man. "You rely too much on your luck," he always told me when he was worried about me.

Family pride was a great thing with us, and we lived in the reflected glory of my grandfather, about whom my father used to talk a great deal. He had been a pasha under the Ottoman Empire, and was widely known as Tahir Pasha the Brave. To modern ears that sounds ridiculous, but in the old days those words were spoken with veneration and awe.

From Pristina, where I was born, 225 miles south of Belgrade, on the present motor highway to Skopje, we moved to Salonika, where we lived not far from the birthplace of Kemal Atatürk, the founder of modern Turkey. An uncle of mine, Major-General Kemal, fought at Atatürk's side.

Later we moved to Istanbul. The Ottoman Empire was shrinking, and each time it shrank we had to move again.

Pristina became Yugoslav and Salonika Greek. With each move my father lost money and property. He could manage property but was incapable of making money. He was a religious teacher, not a businessman.

"Why are we not better off?" I asked him.

"Outward possessions are not the most important things in life," he used to answer.

I took this to be the opinion of an old man estranged from the world.

The family sent me to the Fatih military school, where I was one of many young boys of good family. But I was a black sheep, and my father was asked to take me away.

3

Many of my schoolfellows now have leading positions in Turkey. My brother studied in Germany, three of my cousins obtained prominent positions in the financial administration, and the present mayor of Ankara is a relative of mine.

Neither the times nor my family was to be blamed for the way I went. It was I who broke away from the prescribed paths.

After the First World War armies of occupation came to our country—Italian, French and British. All I was fit for was to be employed by a French transport unit. I learned how to drive, and driving became my passion. A passion for cars has remained with me for the rest of my life.

I drove a lorry into a ditch and smashed it up, and that cost me my job with the French. Then I went to the British for a job, and became driver to a British captain, and drove his Sunbeam. At the driving-wheel I felt myself to be far superior to my contemporaries who were students or were learning a trade or profession. But I was good for nothing.

One day a French officer left his motor-cycle outside my parents' house. Were not the French and British the enemies of Turkey? Was not scoring off them highly enjoyable and, indeed, meritorious? I jumped on the motor-cycle and drove like a maniac down into the city, and then found myself in a street that went steeply downhill, and like many in Istanbul, came to a sudden end before continuing down a flight of steps. After plunging down the latter the motor-cycle was a wreck and I was covered with blood. I was picked up by the Turkish police, who handed me over to the French, who handed me over to the British, in whose

4

service I was. Four sergeants beat me up and put me in a military prison.

I felt I was a martyr. I was a refractory prisoner, and was beaten up again. Did I really hate the British and the French? I imagined I did, but what I really hated was ordinary order and discipline.

A sergeant fetched me from my basement cell and took me upstairs, where he told me to scrub the floor. I grabbed his pistol, forced him to open the door, and fled.

Was I a hero? If so, nobody gave me any credit for it.

Less than an hour later I was caught again, this time by the French, who took me to their *gendarmerie* station in the Babiali district.

During the night I asked to be taken to the lavatory. I climbed through the window and escaped.

During the day I wandered round Istanbul, believing myself to be a rebel, though all I was in reality was a boastful and quarrelsome delinquent of nineteen.

I saw a French soldier lying asleep on a bench on a platform of Yenikapi station. I stole the pistol from his holster, and next day was arrested again.

The list of my offences mounted up—theft, destruction of military property, armed escape from arrest, illegal possession of weapons. . . . They noted in my records that I was a dangerous and determined young criminal.

I was put in solitary confinement, in handcuffs and with my feet in fetters, and I was proud of it.

I was sentenced to three years' imprisonment by a French court-martial. I was taken to Marseilles, and put in a penal labour camp, where I learned the French that in later years earned me compliments from a British ambassador.

The occupying powers concluded a treaty with the new Turkish Government which, among other things, affected the sentences of Turks convicted by them. The result was that a part of my sentence was remitted.

Before going home I stopped at Marseilles, where I got a job at the local works of the Berliet commercial vehicle firm. There I learned something useful for the first time in my life—the locksmith's trade.

Skilled labour was in high demand in Turkey at that time, and I got a job in the transport department of the municipality of Istanbul. Then I became head of the Yozgat fire brigade—and, fool that I was, was proud of it. When I was called up for military service I became a driver to Ali Sait Pasha, the Inspector of the Turkish Army Group I. I believed that to be a career.

Then I decided to make myself independent. One or two successful deals and an advance from my father enabled me to buy an old Studebaker, and I became a taxi-driver on my own account. But the account did not work out—and I was grateful when the Yugoslav Ambassador, Jankovic, took me on as his driver-servant.

I thus became what everybody becomes who has never learned a job and has nothing behind him but his wits—a *kavass*.

The *kavass* Elyesa Bazna: in Turkey anyone who serves a foreigner is known as a *kavass*, a term used especially for servants at foreign embassies. An Ambassador's "personal *kavass*" is his valet, and there are also cleaning *kavasses*, porter *kavasses*, driver *kavasses* and messenger *kavasses*. A *kavass* is an insignificant nobody, and I have always hated being a nobody.

6

I served as *kavass* with Jankovic, with Colonel Class of
the United States Embassy, with Herr Jenke, Counsellor
of the German Embassy, with Mr. Busk, First Secretary of
the British Embassy, and finally with Sir Hughe Knatchbull-Hugessen.

Were they not right to regard me as an utterly insignificant person of obscure origin?

I remember asking myself such a question in April, 1943,
as I sat in the lounge of the Ankara Palace Hotel. The
lounge was furnished with small, old-fashioned tables and
uncomfortable seats. The parquet flooring creaked horribly
when you walked on it. But it was the best hotel in the
place, and I regarded it as a desirable background for myself. In my free time I used to go there and order myself
black coffee and sweet liqueurs. I read the international
newspapers and the waiters treated me like a gentleman.

What might be called the turning point of my life took
place in that lounge. That day I took stock of my life—and
it was a depressing experience. I was thirty-eight, and it
looked as if all that lay ahead of me was a continuation of
the boring, stupid, contemptible life of a *kavass*. In other
words, I was a failure.

It was a bitter reckoning. I entrenched myself behind a
newspaper but I was incapable of taking in the print. I realised that life was slipping away between my fingers, and
that in sitting here amid all this grandeur and trying to behave like a gentleman among his equals all I was doing was
deceiving myself. I asked myself questions, and the answers
that honesty forced from me made me despise myself still
further.

7

Why had I become a *kavass*? Because there was nothing else that I was capable of, nothing else that I could do, except tinker with cars. When I was driver-valet to Jankovic, the Yugoslav Ambassador, there had been a gleam of hope, but it faded out.

"Elyesa," he told me once, "I've heard you singing while washing the car. You have a fine voice, you ought to have it trained."

So I went to the Conservatoire twice a week. My teacher was Professor Klein, a German, and music became my consolation.

I married. Was I in love with my wife? I do not know. I am a Muslim, and was brought up in the old ways that still survive in the Anatolian countryside away from the big towns. A woman's role, according to the Turkish tradition, is to work and give birth to innumerable children, thus fulfilling her only *raison d'être*. I was indifferent to my wife, but I was fond of the children. I brought a camera and photographed them. I showed the photographs to Jankovic. "You're a wonderful photographer," he said.

His praise left me cold. I did not realise that my ability to take good photographs was to bring me near to achieving my dreams.

I worked as chauffeur to the Yugoslav Ambassador for seven years. I did my work, took singing lessons, and photographed my children; and I was consumed with ambition to become a great singer.

When I thought I had made sufficient progress to be able to appear in public I handed in my notice and gave a concert at the Union Française in Istanbul. It was a failure. The songs of the great European composers do not mean anything to my countrymen.

Once more I became a *kavass*, this time with Colonel Class, the American Military Attaché. Did that introduce me to the ways of international society? Was it there that I was shown how to walk on slippery parquet flooring? Colonel Class was a *bon viveur*. His wife was young and pretty, a gentle creature with a passion for poker and gardening. This job did not last too long, and I next became *kavass* to Herr Jenke, the Counsellor at the German Embassy, whose wife was a sister of Ribbentrop. I worked in Herr Jenke's private residence from 1942 until the beginning of 1943. I did not shrink from poking my nose into my employer's correspondence, both private and official. As a *kavass* I could not help it. If you once start snooping, it becomes a passion, a vice. I photographed one or two letters for the sole purpose of showing off to my wife, showing her how completely at home I was in the Jenke household, in spite of the war and spy scares. I lay on the sofa in the drawing-room with my feet on the cushions and a newspaper in my hand and photographed myself in that position —a *kavass* lounging in the drawing-room while his master was out. I told my wife that I wanted to have that kind of drawing-room myself.

The next thing that happened was that one day I noticed that the trunk in my room had been ransacked. Had it been discovered that I secretly read my master's correspondence? Did they think I was a spy?

Herr Jenke informed me that unfortunately he must dispense with my services; he could no longer afford a personal servant. He was very polite, and I took my departure. I was annoyed and upset; I was hurt at obviously having been taken for a spy. Had I not always done my work conscientiously? Had I not worked harder than in any of my previous jobs? When I entered Jenke's service I weighed just under twelve stone; when I was sacked I weighed just over ten.

Sitting in the lounge of the Ankara Palace Hotel on that April afternoon in 1943, I summed up my life. I was a person of no consequence, a person whose life consisted of being ordered about, who washed cars, served cocktails, ran baths for attractive women, read his master's correspondence, and could be thrown out at a moment's notice if the latter chose to regard him as a spy. It was not a cheerful picture.

I had been staring at the newspaper without seeing it. I had been drawing up a balance-sheet of my life, and the results could not have been more depressing. But perhaps if I had not sunk so low, my lot would never have changed; because suddenly, out of the midst of all this gloom, there came an electrifying idea.

This idea startled me out of my bitter brooding. Might it not yet be possible for my wildest dreams to be fulfilled? Why had the Germans suspected me? Because Ankara was neutral soil, where the representatives of the great hostile Powers lived in close proximity, keeping each other under continual observation and setting their agents on each other's trail.

Why not set up as a spy? The idea fascinated me and would not let me go. I made up my mind that I would do it, and sell my services more dearly than anyone else did. I made up my mind to be the greatest spy of all. I saw suddenly that I was in a strong position. I was inconspicuous, retiring, and patient—I was a *kavass*.

Fate showed me the way. My eyes suddenly took in something at which they had been staring unseeingly in the newspaper in front of me. It was an advertisement, and it said: *Driver wanted for First Secretary of British Embassy*.

I walked out of the lounge of the Ankara Palace Hotel in a state of high excitement.

I went carefully through my references, and picked out those from the Yugoslav Ambassador and the American Military Attaché. I did not take the excellent reference given me by the Counsellor at the German Embassy. A German reference of that kind would hardly appeal to an Englishman in wartime.

The house mentioned in the advertisement was in the ambassadorial quarter in the hilly Cancaya district, and lay in the middle of a big, carefully tended garden. A sloping path led to the entrance. Outside there was a Chevrolet with a British Embassy number-plate. I rang the bell.

A maid led me to a room where I had to wait for a long time. Sir Douglas Busk is now British Ambassador in Venezuela. At that time, when he was First Secretary in Ankara, he had not yet been knighted.

I rose respectfully when he came into the room. He was a tall man and, I thought, rather delicate-looking. His eyes rested on me coolly and appraisingly.

"So you are applying for the job?"

"*Oui, monsieur.*"

I answered in French the questions he put to me in English.

"You don't speak English?"

"I can read and understand it, but I speak it only with difficulty."

After that he spoke to me in French.

"Do you know any other languages?"

He indicated that I should sit down again, but I waited until he had taken a seat himself.

I told him that in addition to Turkish and French I could speak Serbo-Croat, a little Greek, and also had a smattering of German.

"References?"

He had a rather abrupt way of asking for information. He was a type with whom I might easily have picked a quarrel if I could have afforded to.

I silently handed him my references.

"How did you manage to pick up such excellent French?"

I told him that as a young man I had lived in Marseilles, where I had worked at the Berliet commercial vehicle works. What I told him was only part of the truth. Actually, I obtained my command of French while I was in prison; but that had nothing to do with Mr. Busk.

He read carefully through my references.

"So you are an experienced driver?" he muttered.

"Yes."

He rose to his feet. "Come over here, please."

I followed him to a desk in a corner of the room. He handed me a pen, and indicated ink-pot and paper. "Write something," he said.

"In French?"

"As you prefer."

I wrote: "My name is Elyesa Bazna. I was born on July 28, 1904, at Pristina. At that time Pristina was still part of

12

the Ottoman Empire. My father, Hafiz Yasar, was a Muslim religious teacher. At the time of the Balkan wars, when we Turks were expelled from Albania and Macedonia, my family emigrated by way of Salonika to Constantinople. . . ."

This was the introduction to the full account of my career, for which I had often been asked when applying for jobs.

"I only wanted to see whether you could write," said Mr. Busk.

"*Oui, monsieur,*" I answered quietly.

He picked up what I had written and took it over towards the window. He examined my hand-writing very carefully; he seemed to be something of a graphologist.

"Hmm—not bad," he said.

I bowed slightly.

"I'll call you Elyesa," he said.

I concluded from this familiarity that I was accepted as his *kavass.*

"Besides driving and looking after the car, there will also be housework for you to do."

In my capacity as *kavass* I was used to being a sort of maid-of-all-work.

"May I know what you propose to pay me, *monsieur?*" I asked.

"One hundred pounds Turkish a month," he replied.

This was a very low wage.

"I am very much obliged to you, *monsieur,*" I said.

Next day I moved into the small room I was to occupy with my few personal possessions.

My duties included dusting and tidying eleven rooms. I

also had to drive and look after the car, besides looking after Mr. Busk's clothes and repairing the central heating apparatus for the following winter. I was responsible for Mr. Busk's personal well-being, and later I also acted as chauffeur to Mrs. Busk, who was a good-looking blonde. When guests were entertained I waited at table, served cocktails, and made coffee. In fact, I was kept constantly on the go.

Mr. Busk was an ambitious man and worked hard. He used to bring files home from the Embassy and work on them in the evening.

I soon found out where he kept them. One day he was called away unexpectedly and apparently slipped the file he was reading into a drawer with the intention of locking it up—he was most meticulous about such things as a rule—but his attention must have been distracted and he had forgotten to do so. It was my habit when he was out to visit his study and see if by chance anything had been left lying about. On this occasion I tried the drawer automatically. To my surprise it opened and there was a file. I immediately slipped it under my livery. I had hardly had time to do so when Mr. Busk walked into the room.

"Has there been a telephone message from Istanbul?" he asked. (At that time Mrs. Busk was in the American Hospital in Istanbul expecting a baby.)

"No, *monsieur*."

I permitted myself a smile. "I can understand *monsieur*. I myself am the father of four children. It is always a very . . ."

He ignored my sympathy.

"Have you finished repairing the central heating?"

"Not yet, *monsieur*."

14

"I hope it won't take long."

"No, *monsieur*," I replied.

I went down to the cellar where the central heating installation was and carefully read through the file.

I had never worried my head very much about war and politics. My experience in my previous positions as *kavass* had left me with a feeling of total indifference to the powerful individuals who went in and out of the Embassies. They were only human, after all, but they made sure, when things went wrong, that it was not they whose fingers got burnt.

I struck the hot water pipes with my tools, and the sound re-echoed throughout the house. There could be no denying my industriousness.

I had put the file down beside me. It contained memoranda written and received at the British Embassy. It gave me a clear picture of the little game in which Turkey, my country, was involved.

I read what Churchill had to say. There was no doubt, in his opinion, that Turkey desired to take part on the winning side in the coming peace conference, and there was no doubt that the winning side was going to be that of the Allies. But the Turks were still afraid of the Germans, and were unwilling to commit themselves. No effort must therefore be spared to persuade Turkey to enter the war in the following spring.

That was what Churchill said. I struck the pipes a series of furious blows. Churchill could of course see the great historical issues, but all I could see was the prospect of wallowing in a muddy trench at the front, being an annoying obstacle in the path of some war-hardened and experienced German unit; and Churchill would never know what the Germans would very likely do to me.

I also discovered from the documents that the Allies wanted to get the Turks to build airfields for them in Turkey. A flood of weapons and war material was to flow into my country. "Specialists must be sought out who will teach the Turks to handle this material."

I decided that for a start it would not be a bad thing if they got hold of a central heating mechanic to relieve the First Secretary of the British Embassy of having to depend on a Turkish ignoramus such as myself.

I read of plans to open the way to the Black Sea to establish contact with the Russian southern flank. The Rumanian oilfields could be heavily bombed from bases in Turkey, and oil production at Ploesti crippled.

I paused in my reading of the Allied plans for Turkey and finished repairing the central heating. Then I read another memorandum referring to the conference at Adana. Churchill had spent two days there conferring in a special train with the Turkish President Inönü. It was all, of course, top secret. The Russians, according to the document, had gained victories over the Germans, and the other Allies had operated successfully against the Germans in Africa. But it was precisely this, so Churchill said to President Inönü, that endangered Turkey. The Germans, in pursuance of their traditional *Drang nach Osten*, and impelled by the necessity of assuring their fuel supplies, might well be tempted to attack and invade Turkey, which must therefore be armed and ready to defend herself.

I also read President Inönü's reply. He spoke of the post-

16

war world order. In his opinion Russia would set out on a course of imperialism, and it was necessary for Turkey to be very cautious indeed. The real threat to her had always come not from the Germans, but from the Russians. After the Germans had been beaten, all the defeated countries would be Bolshevised, and that, in the Turkish view, was the reality of the situation.

A long time afterwards I had an opportunity of reading this extract from a telegram of Stalin's to Churchill:

". . . the international situation in Turkey remains very ticklish. On the one hand Turkey has concluded a pact of neutrality and friendship with the U.S.S.R. and a treaty of mutual assistance in the event of aggression with Great Britain; on the other hand there is the treaty of friendship with Germany which Turkey signed only three days before the German attack on the Soviet Union. It is not clear to me how Turkey in these circumstances proposes to reconcile her undertakings towards the U.S.S.R. and Great Britain on the one hand and her undertaking towards Germany on the other. . . ."

Whatever the powers-that-be might think of Turkey, I, as I obtained this overall view of the world situation while working away on the central heating system in the cellar, decided that it would be a bad business to get involved in this war, whether as a partner of Britain or as a victim of Germany. For a few moments my mind was filled with grandiose thoughts. Something like idealism overcame me. I decided that, if I betrayed the British plans to the Germans, the latter would be able to checkmate them without having to waste their strength on attacking Turkey; and Turkey, I thought, when it saw the British moves checked by the Germans, would hesitate before involving herself in war on the Allied side. Thus I would be serving the cause of my country's neutrality.

I packed up my tools, hid the file under my jacket, and felt myself to be the unrecognised centre of a world at war.

I went upstairs. Mr. Busk came out of his study. He looked at me and I felt my heart beating against the file.

With difficulty I forced myself to show no trace of emotion, and said: "The central heating is now in order. . . ."

He did not give me time to finish the sentence.

"I've just had a telephone call from Istanbul," he said. "You can congratulate me on the birth of a daughter."

I bowed. When I looked at him again there was a smile on my face.

"Permit me to congratulate you very heartily, *monsieur*," I said.

He nodded, and dashed away.

I went into his study and put the file back where it came from.

During the next few weeks only one female in the world, apart from his wife, existed for Mr. Busk. That was his little daughter, newly born in Istanbul. The female in whom I became interested, however, was the nurse whom Mrs. Busk brought back to Ankara with the baby.

The nurse's name was Mara. She was in her young thirties, was slender, and had black hair; and she seemed to me to combine the best characteristics of the women of several nationalities. She had the bright blue eyes of a Swede; her sensitive mouth reminded me of the south of

18

France; and her delicate hands and fingers and the graceful way she moved them reminded me of the women of Bucharest. Her origins were rather obscure, but her willingness to be affectionate was evident. Later I discovered that she was a heavy smoker and was very fond of whisky. When she drank her laughter was gay and infectious, she flashed her white teeth, and her voice betrayed a great deal of unscrupulousness and taste for adventure. There was also something about her that suggested the wind and the sea. Perhaps this was the heritage of an American sailor on her mother's side.

I was married and had four children. My wife lived with the children in Istanbul; I sent her money and tried not to think about her, and in the end I managed to forget her. I was disgusting, but I did not care—I was living in a dream world. I quickly fell for Mara.

The first time I saw her, her eyes were full of grief and sorrow. I overheard Mrs. Busk telling her husband that Mara would very likely be staying with them for some time. She had just had an unhappy love affair; her engagement had just been broken off.

Mrs. Busk told her husband this one day while I was serving tea and Mr. Busk was gazing entranced at the baby in its cot. The impression prevailed that my knowledge of English was very limited, with the result that Mr. and Mrs. Busk would sometimes talk of their affairs in front of me. I smiled at the baby, waved two fingers at it, and withdrew.

I went to Mara, looked at her seriously and said: "Can I help you? Who has done you wrong?"

Her eyes grew big and inquiring.

"What do you know?" she said.

I shook my head.

"I know nothing," I said. "But I feel you are unhappy."

It became clear to me that I could not get what I wanted in the Busk household. My objective was the British Embassy itself. As all the *kavasses* in all the foreign embassies in Ankara knew, the Ambassador, Sir Hughe Knatchbull-Hugessen, was looking for a valet. This was a much-sought-after position. I decided that the best course would be to secure a recommendation to His Excellency—from his First Secretary, Mr. Busk, for instance. This would be far better than applying for the job direct.

I arranged to meet Mara in a little park between Cancaya and Kavaklidere.

This was the first time I had ever been there. I am not fond of going for walks.

"It's delightful here, I often come here," I said. "I like being alone. It's a delightful place to meditate in."

I did not look at Mara, but at the trees and bushes, in which I was not interested.

"Do you like nature?" she asked softly.

I did not answer, but thought about the next step.

A few moments later she said: "You felt that I was unhappy."

"If it was a man who let you down, forget him," I quietly replied. "Don't seek any cheap consolation. What you must do is find a way back to yourself, that's all."

I told her that in the old days there had been vineyards here. That was why the most popular Turkish wine was still called Kavaklidere, though now, as she could see, there were no vines for miles around.

I had picked up this piece of information from the wine-list at the Ankara Palace, on which such titbits are recorded for the benefit of tourists.

"What a lot of things you know," she said.

I smiled wanly. "All I know is that I am going to give Mr. Busk notice," I said.

She looked at me in astonishment. "Why?" she exclaimed. "He's very satisfied with you."

"I'm leaving because of you," I coolly replied.

She did not know what to make of this remark, but the grief in her eyes lessened. "I don't understand," she murmured eventually.

"Never mind, it doesn't matter," I said. "Don't bother your head about me, I must leave you now, I've got to go. Forgive me." I walked away without casting her another glance.

Mara was impatient by nature. On the evening of the second day after this conversation she insisted on a short meeting—"in our park," she said. At first I said no, but I let her go on insisting, and in the end I gave in. In her eyes there was an expression of full comprehension.

We sat on a bench, and I put the evening newspaper between us.

"Why do you want to leave?" she asked.

"You know," I replied.

"No, I don't," she said.

"Every woman knows that sort of thing without being told."

"Tell me all the same."

I told her I was married, but had felt attracted to her

from when I first set eyes on her. I said:

"I'm convinced that you must have an unhappy love affair behind you. I feel it. That will make it easier for you to understand why I must keep out of your way. That's why I'm going to hand in my notice."

One word led to another, our hands touched, and one little act of intimacy led to the next. We assured each other that we would respect each other's feelings and agreed that we must renounce each other, but we were already under the spell of an irresistible mutual attraction.

"Mara, you misunderstand me," I said. She laid her head on my shoulder and nodded.

"There is one possibility," I said.

"What?"

"I can't live in the same house with you. But the Ambassador is looking for a valet. Why shouldn't you have a frank talk with Mrs. Busk? Why shouldn't you tell her that you and I don't want to make each other unhappy? She'll understand. Mr. Busk may recommend me to the Ambassador. He won't like it at all if two of his staff keep meeting secretly."

"We might be able to see each other occasionally if you worked for the Ambassador," Mara murmured.

"Do you think that that would be a good thing for us?" I asked.

Mara hugged me to her.

"I'll talk to Mrs. Busk," she murmured.

If Mrs. Busk passed any of this on to Mr. Busk, he showed no sign of it in his behaviour to me. I felt sure that the prospect of losing my services suited him. I had noticed that he was very careful with his money, and in recent weeks he had obviously been doubting whether he was justified in spending it on my wages. The central heating was repaired, and the work could be done by female labour which was even cheaper than mine.

A few days later he asked me whether I should be interested in becoming the Ambassador's valet.

"I should naturally feel very fortunate to secure such a position, *monsieur*," I said. "But I hope I have done nothing to cause you dissatisfaction, *monsieur?*"

He ignored this remark.

"The decision rests with Sir Hughe, of course," he said. "He wants to see you. Be ready to come with me to the Embassy in half an hour."

I left Mr. Busk's study and took a hot bath in Mrs. Busk's bathroom, which I always liked to use if the coast happened to be clear. It was risky, but less so than in most houses because of the way the rooms were arranged.

CHAPTER **2**

It was pleasant to lie in the bath and contemplate my forth-coming encounter with His Excellency the British Am-bassador. I lay back, and the hot water made me feel fine. I always made a point of using Mrs. Busk's delightfully scented bathsalts. I gazed at the shining mirrors and the scent bottles which gave so much pleasure both to me and to Mara, and I dreamt about one day having a luxurious bathroom like this myself.

Mara rubbed my shoulders and the back of my neck. I lay back and enjoyed the play of her fingers.

She told me that the Ambassador was fifty-seven, and a very smart gentleman. He was said to treat his staff very decently.

I listened to her in silence.

I already knew a good deal about Sir Hughe Knatchbull-Hugessen. He was born on March 26, 1886, and was edu-cated at Eton and Oxford. As a young man in the Foreign Office he had had the task of despatching the telegram declaring war on Germany at midnight on August 3, 1914. He had been in Ankara since the end of February, 1939. In between he had served in China, Persia and Belgium.

"They say he plays the piano beautifully, and paints very well too," Mara said.

Men of that type do not tend to be mistrustful.

Mara had very skilfully found out a great deal about the Ambassador from Mrs. Busk.

"Now it's time for you to be off," she said. She hesitated, but then added: "We shall see each other again, shan't we?"

"Of course."

We had grown very intimate. Her duty was to bathe and look after the Busk baby. The attentions she lavished on the baby were shared only by me.

While I carefully dressed myself, she ran off the bath water, and cleaned the bath. She bent down over it, and when she spoke there was a kind of tension in her voice. What she said took my breath away.

"Sometimes I think that you want to be the Ambassador's servant for some quite definite purpose," she said.

I was combing my hair in front of the mirror, and what she said took me so much aback that I found it hard to speak.

"What on earth do you mean?" I answered as calmly as I could.

Mara was now standing erect, and we looked at each other in the mirror.

"You read the documents that Mr. Busk brings home from the Embassy," she said.

I turned and looked at her calmly.

"Have you been going secretly to my room?"

"I went there to see you, and you weren't there. The documents were under the pillow."

So she had been snooping in my room. I did not blame

her. I should have done the same myself.

"Then why didn't you tell Mr. Busk?"

She did not answer. I realised that I had found an ally.

I left the bathroom first. When I had made sure that there was no one about, I beckoned to Mara to follow.

Outside the house Mr. Busk was waiting beside his car.

"You've been dolling yourself up to make a good impression," he said in a slightly irritable manner.

"*Monsieur*," I answered politely, "my beard is so strong that I have to shave twice a day. I should not like to put off His Excellency by any five o'clock shadow."

I opened the car door to let Mr. Busk get in, and then took my place at the steering wheel.

Mara appeared at the front door with the baby in her arms. She took its tiny hand and waved it to Mr. Busk and me as we drove away.

I did everything possible to avoid perspiring. I moved slowly to prevent my hands from trembling. I was afraid. To anyone who looked at me at that moment it ought to have been obvious that I was not to be trusted.

But the Ambassador did not look up when Mr. Busk, his First Secretary, took me into his study. Sir Hughe Knatchbull-Hugessen was not aware that his enemy was being introduced to him. If there is such a thing as a sixth sense, he did not possess it—at any rate in relation to his future valet, who was so much below his social level. For him I was a duster and a clothes-brush. My fear vanished.

"Sir, this is Elyesa . . ." said Mr. Busk.

Sir Hughe looked up briefly, nodded, and beckoned to

Mr. Busk to approach him. He handed him a file. They exchanged significant glances; they seemed to be in agreement about the importance of the documents that the file contained.

"I'll let you have them back tomorrow morning," Mr. Busk said.

So he was going to take them home. I knew he was going to a party that evening at the Soviet Commercial Attaché's; I had pressed his dinner jacket in preparation for the event that morning.

Mr. Busk put the documents in his brief-case. I did not look at him, and he walked out of the room. I looked forward to reading the contents of the brief-case that evening.

I stood, as if frozen, on the expensive carpet, ready to submit to inspection by my future master. It was a big room with a high ceiling, and it was tastefully furnished. There was a tasteful carpet, tasteful club furniture and a tasteful desk with a tasteful gentleman behind it, who did not cough but cleared his throat, did not laugh but smiled, never clenched his fists but carefully laid his hands over each other. He was slender, with a slim face, a high, pale brow and an elegant moustache. If he ever discovered my deception he would be mildly offended; only if he found a speck of dust on his sleeve would he lose his temper.

Quietly he asked me about my previous jobs. I told him exactly what I had told Mr. Busk, naturally omitting to mention that I had once worked for Ribbentrop's brother-in-law.

He relied on his First Secretary's recommendation, so the interview was brief.

"When can you begin?" he asked. He had a pleasant, soft

27

voice. Undoubtedly he sometimes sang romantic songs when he sat by the piano.

"Right away, your Excellency," I replied.

The butler, whose name was Zeki, showed me over the house. The Ambassador's residence lay among the hills of Cancaya. It was a big building, an English country house on the edge of the Anatolian steppe. The Embassy proper was next door, but I found out that Sir Hughe preferred working in his own study in the Ambassador's residence. Apparently he also kept secret papers there.

His study was on the first floor, immediately over the kitchen. The first thing that struck me was that the carpet would muffle the sound of my footsteps. Nobody would hear me moving about in his study in his absence.

The staff quarters, including the modest little room which was allotted to me, were on the ground floor near the kitchen.

I took note of the distances between the rooms. There were long corridors on each floor. There were two staircases, so I should be able to choose which to use. On the ground floor were two paintings, one of King George VI and the other of the Queen. Whichever way I hurried back to my room one of the paintings would lie on my path. In case of need I might be able to hide things behind one or other of them.

On the second floor were the separate bedrooms of Sir Hughe and his wife, as well as that of their daughter, and their respective bathrooms. I found out that without hurrying it took me just under a minute to go from the Ambassador's bathroom to his bedroom, and nearly three minutes from the bathroom to his study on the floor below. From there to my room took about two minutes. I felt sure His Excellency was the kind of man who very much enjoyed his bath. In that I resembled him, though he might be offended at being put on a level with me. The second thing that struck me was that, as it was part of my duty to run his bath and help him dress afterwards, there would be time for me to lay my hands on the key of the safe which he otherwise always kept about his person.

The butler handed over to my care the bedroom and the ambassadorial wardrobe. Then he left me alone.

In the cupboard I found twenty-five suits, including uniforms. I have a weakness for good cloth, and I stroked Sir Hughe's suits appreciatively. A barely perceptible trace of sharp perfume emerged from the wardrobe. My fingers slid into the pockets, and I found some indigestion tablets.

On the dressing-table there lay an unfinished pen-drawing of the view from the window, which overlooked the city down below. I admired the skill with which it was done. Sir Hughe was an artist.

With the drawing still in my hand, I went over to the window and opened it. I drew a deep breath. In Ankara autumn is the most beautiful season of the year. The fierce, parching, paralysing heat of summer is over, the sky is dark blue, the temperature mild, and the cool evening air delicious.

I looked down towards the poplars at the foot of the hill and noticed the tennis courts that belonged to the Embassy. If Sir Hughe took exercise there, that would give me another opportunity to carry out my purpose. That was the third thing that struck me.

I put down the drawing and closed the window. I went

over to the bedside table and opened the drawer. It contained sleeping pills, another discovery that gave me pleasure. I closed the drawer again.

When I turned a beautiful woman was standing in the doorway. She had big, bright eyes. Her hair was combed closely over her head, and the corners of her mouth were turned sceptically downwards.

"Are you the new valet?"

I bowed.

"Yes, madam. My name is Elyesa." Lady Knatchbull-Hugessen looked at me briefly, and walked silently out of the room. I felt I should have to be more on my guard with her than with her husband. Fear rose in me again.

To give myself courage, when I left the bedroom I took the pen-drawing with me. I hid it on the ground floor behind the picture of King George VI. Not till three days later did I fish it out again and put it back on the dressing-table. His Excellency had neither missed it nor noticed its reappearance. He just looked at it vaguely.

He certainly also wrote poetry. I felt immeasurably superior to him.

Mara was as inflammable as tinder. All thought of her ex-fiancé was discarded like an old coat. Her arms were twined round my neck more often than my fourteen ties, and she seemed to have more arms than an octopus. Her imagination in thinking out new ways of demonstrating her affection was inexhaustible. She also excelled herself in the preparation of my favourite dishes—*imam bayildi* for instance, which means "the *imam* fainted" and consists of eggs and fruit cooked in olive oil and eaten cold with tomatoes and onions, or *cerkes tavugu*, which is chicken cooked in the

Cherkassian manner, very sharp, and a real delicacy. That evening she made me a *baklava*, a sweet made with almonds, pistachio nuts or walnuts.

We were in the Busk kitchen. The baby lay sleeping in its cot. Its parents were at the Soviet Commercial Attaché's.

I watched Mara's skilful fingers preparing the *baklava*. The electric lamp shone coldly and brightly; it was the brightest in the house.

"It's so nice to have you here," said Mara.

I rose, picked up a tray, and told her I would be back in a minute. I hurried out of the kitchen and through the dark house.

Mr. Busk had his habits, and I knew them. I found what I wanted in the drawers of his desk, opening which had ceased to cause me any trouble. I took out his brief-case and removed from it the documents he had brought home. I put the brief-case back in the desk, put the documents on the tray, and covered them with a napkin. I knew where the bottle of brandy was, and I took it and two glasses down to the kitchen.

"That's fine!" Mara exclaimed when she saw it.

Her only disappointment was that it was not whisky. I put it down, removed the napkin, and laid the tray on the table right under the light.

Mara stopped busying herself with the *baklava* and stared at me open-mouthed. I went to where the saucepans were hanging over the hearth, and from one of them took my Leica. It was an old one, which I had previously used only for taking photographs of my children.

I photographed the documents page by page. I had to climb on to a kitchen stool to be able to photograph them vertically from above. This procedure was efficient but

31

complicated, and it was undignified. I realised that I must think up a better way of doing the job.

"I knew it," Mara muttered.

I took no notice of her, but concentrated on taking good, sharp pictures.

"Do you want Turkey to be dragged into the war?" I said casually. "I'm sure you don't!" She did not reply.

I went on working coolly and confidently. For this I had to thank Mara. In her presence I found it easy to be cool and confident. Doing all this in her presence prevented fear from getting the better of me.

When I had finished I put the camera back in the saucepan, took the documents and the untouched brandy back to the study, and carefully put everything back exactly where I had found it.

When I got back to the kitchen Mara was still gazing at the saucepan in which I had hidden the camera.

"Nobody would ever have found it there!" she whispered.

"There's no reason to whisper," I said.

I had hidden the camera in the saucepan only half an hour previously in case the Busks came home unexpectedly.

Mara was in a state of high excitement, and her nervousness gave me the strength to be calm and collected. I smiled, and she took me to be the hero that she wanted me to be.

"Don't forget the *baklava*," I said calmly.

"You belong to the Turkish secret service!" she exclaimed excitedly.

I smiled, and did not stop smiling. I was the secret service personified—cold-blooded, supercilious and, above all, secret.

I lounged nonchalantly over the kitchen table, underneath which, however, as a result of delayed shock, my knees were trembling violently.

I had had no time to read the documents I had photographed. I discovered their contents only later.

Included in them was a memorandum in which the British listed the American war material so far delivered to the Russians. This included:

189,000 field telephones
670,000 miles of cable
45,000 tons of barbed wire
10,500 tons of leather
4,000,000 pairs of boots
4,100 aircraft
2,000 tanks
150,000 sub-machine guns. . . .

The list was endless. When it came into German possession it would show them the enormous effort that the Allies were making to support each other.

Moreover, the memorandum mentioned a conference which had taken place in Moscow, in October 1943. It said that the Russians were going to press for Turkish intervention in the war against Germany. "Vyshinsky had already explained that such action on the Turkish part would cause fifteen German divisions to be withdrawn from the eastern front."

Mara served the *baklava*, which we ate with relish. I had laid a spell of high adventure over the girl, and that tiny morsel of British life, the Busk baby, lay asleep in the cot beside us.

"What I find so stimulating about this work is the danger," I remarked.

I also remarked: "I sometimes find it revolting to deceive people. But it is so wonderful to have you."

Another observation that I let slip was: "I am doing all this for my country."

By saying all these things, I increased my sense of my own importance and that of my mission.

"Do you love me?" Mara said. That was the only question she asked.

"Yes," I answered, and believed it.

I was shameless, and at the same time I was unsure of myself. I was full of greed for my objective, and full of fear of the path that I must follow to achieve it.

When I left Mr. Busk's house Mara took the camera from the saucepan and handed it to me as if it were a love-gift that I must not look at until just before I fell asleep, so that I might think of her tenderly as I did so.

The night was noticeably cold. I turned up my coat collar and hurried away.

I started work as Sir Hughe Knatchbull-Hugessen's valet next morning.

I lived in a kind of trance. My own shadow was always behind me, driving me on. Every morning at seven-thirty I awakened the Ambassador with a glass of orange juice. It was my shadow that bent over my shoulder and tried to discover British secrets on his bedside table.

On the bedside table there lay a black leather box, rather like an attaché case.

My next task was to run the Ambassador's morning bath. He always stayed in bed for half an hour after awakening,

34

reading newspapers or papers that he took from the black box.

When he went to the bathroom he told me which suit he wanted to wear that day. I would take it from the wardrobe, make sure that the buttons were all right, and press it if it were creased.

I went to the bedside table and tried the black box, but it was locked.

When the Ambassador went down to breakfast I had to take the box to his study, where it was taken from me by his private secretary.

The Ambassador took twenty minutes over his breakfast. He spent twenty-five minutes over lunch and at most half an hour over dinner. His ways were so regular that you could have set your watch by them.

After lunch he always played the piano in the drawing-room for an hour and a half. Before dinner he took another bath, while I laid out his dinner jacket. He and his wife and daughter always changed for dinner.

I adapted myself to the rhythm of life in this household. While the family was at meals I had nothing to do. Waiting at table was Mustafa's business. I had to help Mustafa only when Sir Hughe and Lady Knatchbull-Hugessen had company.

I observed Mustafa carefully. He was a carefree, submissive, cheerful, unreflective sort of person. Nothing ever surprised him, and if I had stunned Sir Hughe in his presence and dragged him out of the Embassy, he would merely have shrugged his shoulders and assumed that there was a good reason for what I was doing.

Manoli Filoti, the chef, was quite a different type. He

was an artist at cooking steaks, and had a tremendous idea of his own importance. He set about the pots and pans like Toscanini setting about an orchestra, imposing a diminuendo here, bringing a *shashlik* solo to life there, and, whenever he took a finished roast *opus* from the oven, he seemed to be expecting a burst of tumultuous applause from an enthusiastic audience.

He regarded himself as Lady Knatchbull-Hugessen's right hand, and, not satisfied with his little world of softly boiled breakfast eggs and calves' livers *flambés*, assumed the additional duty of keeping a watchful eye on us other *kavasses*.

He had a room next to mine but, to my relief, he did not spend the night there. He had a family and a flat in the city. He must certainly have got on his wife's nerves every evening by describing in detail how he had solved yet another British imperial problem in the kitchen.

Zeki, the butler, was the personification of dignity and nothing else. He regarded everything below the level of his own elevated nose with complete contempt. He was much too occupied with keeping his head erect to have time to take any notice of me.

Those were the members of the domestic staff with whom I came into contact, and it was they who would notice how I behaved.

The Ambassador's private secretary was named Louise. She was a nice woman, and the soul of dependability, like the safe that stood in her office. I took careful note of the safe but smiled at Miss Louise, as if I were interested only in her. She responded calmly and coolly, and took from me the black leather box which the Ambassador had handed to me in his bedroom.

Miss Louise opened the safe, and I realised that there was a regular, daily routine connected with the key. In the daytime, during office hours, it was in her charge. At night the Ambassador took charge of it himself.

Miss Louise put the black box in the safe, next to a number of red boxes which were in it already.

After two days in the ambassadorial residence I had discovered the purpose of this system of red and black boxes. They were necessary because of Sir Hughe's very definite temperamental peculiarities, from which he never departed.

All documents, memoranda, telegrams and so forth that required to be brought to his notice or needed his personal attention were put in the red boxes. In other words, the most important documents were put in them. They were brought from the Embassy to the private residence because that was where he preferred working.

Files that were not finished with were left overnight in Miss Louise's safe. But documents on matters about which the Ambassador wanted to think at leisure, about problems over which he wanted to brood, were taken from the red boxes and put in the black box, which Sir Hughe took with him to his bedroom.

I decided that I had made a remarkable discovery. Important but not exceptionally secret documents were kept in the Embassy building under the supervision of a strong force of security guards. But the really vital documents lay during the daytime in the red boxes on the Ambassador's desk in his residence, and during the night they were put in

Louise's safe, which was a very simple one; and the only watch-dog outside the door was a tired security guard, vintage 1894, who showed signs of considerable wear and tear as a result of everlasting night duty and had an ill-fitting denture which whistled when he dozed off to sleep.

The most important documents of all, however, went into the black box on Sir Hughe's bedside table. And he pored over these so passionately until the late hours that it was only with the aid of sleeping pills that he was able to go to sleep.

I realised that I was at the source and fountain-head. The Ambassador's bedroom was my little kingdom.

My room, in the servants' quarters, was small and simply furnished. It contained a bed, a cupboard, a table and a chair. I supplemented this by buying a 100-watt bulb for the bedside lamp. I also bought four metal rods and a metal ring. I could screw my camera to the ring, and the metal rods could be used to support the ring. Thus I had a "tripod" I could use for photographing documents; all I had to do was to lay them between the metal rods. I also devised subsidiary uses for the rods and ring to divert suspicion from their real purpose. I put two rods in the cupboard and hung my ties over them, and I fixed the other two into some boxes I had made and put on the wall near the wash-stand so that they stuck out into the room. I hung my towels and washing things on them, and sometimes I hung socks on them to dry.

For most of the time the metal ring served as an embellishment of my ash-tray. The marks on it made by screwing the camera to it looked like marks made by burning cigarettes.

Last of all I bought a big piece of wax.

Mara was my consolation. When I was with her I wept my heart out. She was so lovely and carefree, and she had such inexhaustible reserves of affection.

"Why can't I be satisfied as I am?" I said to her, as if it were her fault. "I've got the best paid job I've ever had. Why can't I keep my fingers off that other business?"

I was as changeable as the weather. Moods of depression and exhilaration followed each other in rapid succession.

Mara pressed my hand. She felt it her duty to encourage me, because she believed me to be the Turkish patriot I nearly believed myself to be. "I'm so frightened for you, but you must stick to it. You must stick to it. You mustn't give in now!"

She had no idea what she was talking about, but she went on talking all the same. "You're wonderful!" she said. "I know you'll succeed!"

My mood promptly changed. I smiled with vanity and self-satisfaction, and started talking about the Ambassador to whom I was supposed to be loyal.

"You ought to see him first thing in the morning," I said. "He's as limp as a pair of old flannel trousers. But then he pulls himself together. He swallows the orange juice I take him, and his cells fill up again. Then he gets out of bed and has his bath, and when he comes back from the bath-room he's fresh as a daisy and ready for another intellectual day."

"How well you talk!" Mara exclaimed.

39

By now I was well away. I took three pieces of wax from my coat pocket and showed them to her.

"What on earth is that?" she exclaimed.

My inferiority complex came out in a fit of boasting.

"The impressions of a key," I explained to her contemptuously.

I told her how I had got them.

His Excellency had been splashing about contentedly in his bath while I was laying out his grey suit in the bedroom. He had left his keys on the bedside table, the key of the safe and the keys to the red boxes and the black box.

Quickly I took the impressions.

I left a little bit of wax sticking to the keys. I went over to the cupboard, took one of Sir Hughe's silk handkerchiefs, cleaned the keys with it, and put the key-ring back on the bedside table.

At that moment he came in in his bath-robe. He appeared so suddenly that I had no time to be frightened.

I held up the handkerchief appraisingly, turned and noticed His Excellency. The handkerchief was snow white.

"It ought to be sent to the laundry, Your Excellency," I said.

He nodded, but he was not really listening. To his immense relief he saw his keys lying on the bedside table. He picked them up, put them in his bath-gown pocket, and walked out again.

A moment later I heard him gargling. I wiped my brow with the fine silk handkerchief.

I went on bragging to Mara. "You ought to hear him gargling," I said. "It's a real coloratura gargle."

I looked with amusement at the wax impressions. I imagined how startled Sir Hughe must have been when he suddenly realised in the bath that he had left his top secret key-ring lying about. He must have popped out of the bath like a flash.

I grinned superciliously, and said to Mara: "Sir Hughe is too well-bred. If he hadn't wasted time putting on his bathrobe, he would have caught me red-handed."

I sat with Mara on a bench in the little park of Kavaklidere. She snuggled close to me and whispered: "Do you know what I sometimes wish?"

I was bored, and told her that I hadn't the slightest idea.

She sighed. "I wish we had a little house in which we could be alone and happy."

"If all goes well, we shall soon have a little house like that," I murmured.

This caused her to embrace me so passionately that it distracted me from what I was thinking about. I rose to my feet.

"When is Mr. Busk going to another party?" I asked in a matter-of-fact voice.

"The day after tomorrow."

On the evening when Mr. Busk went to his party I went to see Mara. I found a list of names in his desk, and photographed it in the kitchen.

I spent the night in Mara's room. We were very happy, though we had to be very quiet.

The camera was in the pocket of my overcoat, hanging over the end of the bed. I had photographed the list of names of all the British secret agents in Turkey.

41

At first light I crept out of the house. It was October 26, 1943. This was to be the decisive day. I had decided to approach the German Embassy that evening.

I too was now looking forward to the little house of which Mara had spoken.

I had taken altogether fifty-two photographs, and I pondered over the price I should ask for them. That day I kept as far as possible out of Sir Hughe's way. The thought of the money dazzled me, and I had to hold myself firmly in hand.

I decided to ask for £20,000 sterling. I was intoxicated at the thought of such a large sum of money. It did not for a moment enter my head that the Germans would refuse.

I should have to approach them confidently, and forget that only six months previously I had been *kavass* to Herr Jenke, the Counsellor at the Embassy. It was absolutely vital that they should trust me. They must believe me to be a spy, to have always been a spy. I must create the impression of having laid my plans well in advance.

I waited impatiently to go off duty. October 26 was the longest day of my life.

I left the British Embassy at six o'clock, with the films in my pocket.

The porter-*kavass* at the German Embassy was named Peter, he was a Yugoslav and he recognised me.

"Do you want to come back and work here again?" he asked.

"Maybe I do," I replied.

I could hardly contain my excitement. By now it was

seven o'clock. I had spent a whole hour trying vainly to calm myself.

"Please tell Frau Jenke I should like to see her," I said.

The German Embassy was in the Atatürk Boulevard. It was a little world of its own. Outside the wrought iron gates were rattling motor-cars, men driving donkeys, barefoot peasants on a visit to town, beggars, unpaved streets, noise, din, the hooting of motor-horns. Inside the gate was order, quiet, scrupulous cleanliness, trees, a carefully tended lawn and flower beds; an attractive scene.

The British and German Embassies were the most impressive buildings in Ankara. The idea that the kavass Elyesa Bazna was about to be deeply concerned with both made me smile. It was such an amusing idea that it calmed my nerves.

Peter had been telephoning. He looked at me.

"They want you to go across," he said.

I knew the way.

The house in which the Jenkes lived was next door to the Embassy building. It was built in oriental style. I was received by a kavass who was a stranger to me; perhaps he was my successor with Herr Jenke.

He took me into the drawing-room and left me.

I had to wait for a long time. I sat on the sofa, on which I had photographed myself taking my ease some months before. The room was just as it had been when I used to dust it. There were distinct feminine touches about it. Frau Jenke, Ribbentrop's sister, had furnished it—deep, soft, comfortable easy chairs, heavy curtains, carpets in which your feet sank.

I rose and drew the curtains. I switched on both the

43

standard lamps and sat in one of the armchairs. My face was in the shadow.

I had to wait for a long time.

I put my hands in my pockets and clutched my rolls of film.

Inge Jenke was a nervous, ambitious woman in her middle forties. She had not always been easy to get on with. Now I know that she died later from Parkinson's disease. Perhaps the German Foreign Minister's sister was already ill and unhappy. But, if she was, she never let me, the *kavass*, see it.

She came into the room, and I rose.

"*Bonsoir, madame*," I murmured.

She looked at me.

"Why did you draw the curtains, Elyesa?" she asked.

"Madam," I said, "I hope to get a great deal of money from you. . . ."

Not a flicker of surprise appeared on her face. However extraordinary she may have thought my behaviour, she did not betray it.

"I am afraid that I haven't got very much time for you," she said.

"Shall we sit down, madam?" I asked quietly.

A very alert expression appeared in her eyes.

"No, Elyesa, we shan't sit down. I think it would be better if you left immediately."

I ignored this remark, and said: "I have just come from the British Embassy, madam. I wanted to tell you that I am now Sir Hughe Knatchbull-Hugessen's valet. I have come to see you here, madam, probably at the risk of my life. . . ."

She leant forward, as if the better to grasp the import of what I was saying.

For a moment there was silence. The palms of my hands grew moist.

Eventually she said slowly: "I think my husband will wish to see you."

I remained in the shadow of the lamps. I was too exhausted to feel triumphant.

CHAPTER 3

I had once read some letters that Albert Jenke received
from his brother-in-law Ribbentrop and, though he did not
say so, I knew well enough that that was why he had
sacked me. Now, on the evening of October 26, 1943, I
was going to see him for the first time since then. But I
had no time to feel any embarrassment.

After Inge Jenke left the room to fetch her husband, I
waited patiently.

Eventually the two appeared together. I had the impression that Jenke wanted his wife there, so that she
would be able to corroborate what passed.

"Good evening, Elyesa," he said.

I could not tell how interested he was in what I was going
to say. He was a businessman, and waited to hear my proposition.

He was a man of nearly fifty, and not a professional
diplomatist. His father was German and his mother Swiss.
His father enjoyed a certain celebrity in Turkey, where he
had built a dam across a valley. Albert Jenke had also been
in the contracting business, and had lived for many years
in Istanbul. Turkey was his second home. But for his mar-

46

riage into the Ribbentrop family he would never have been invited to join the diplomatic service, and he had agreed to do so only after much hesitation.

Earlier, when I had been his servant, he had been a Counsellor in the Embassy, but during the past few days he had been promoted to the rank of Minister and Chargé d'Affaires to the Ambassador, Franz von Papen.

"Mr. Minister, allow me to offer you my hearty congratulations on your promotion," I said politely.

"Thank you," he curtly replied.

He may have thought that this was no business of a *kavass* who had been sacked for unreliability.

To conceal my nervousness I started making a speech. The words flowed from my lips like oil.

"Turkey and Germany have always been on terms of friendship," I said. "The two countries have never fought each other. We Turks still like the Germans, and there has been no change in our attitude. . . ."

The cool expression on his face remained unaltered. What I said was true and unobjectionable, but there were false notes in my voice which made the words hollow and empty.

Jenke was not taking any high-flown idealism from me. A mocking and ironic expression came into his eyes and made me angry. I changed my tone.

"The Germans are not doing so well at the moment that they can afford to refuse help, no matter what quarter it may come from," I said harshly. "I am in a position to take photographs at the British Embassy. With a Leica. To be precise, not with a long-distance lens, but with an ordinary lens. 1: 2 or 1: 1.5. I am offering you the films that I have taken. All the documents that I have photographed so far are marked either 'secret' or 'most secret'. . . ."

He interrupted. He sounded incredulous.

"Have you the films with you?"

My fingers were playing with the rolls of film in my pocket.

"Of course not," I replied. "At the moment I am offering you two films, for which I want £20,000 sterling. If you accept my proposition, each additional film will cost £15,000."

The sums of money that I mentioned shook him. I had managed to startle him out of his reserve.

"You're crazy," he exclaimed.

"Of course you are free to decline the proposition," I said. "The Soviet Embassy is two doors away. The Russians will certainly be prepared to pay well for information about what their allies are up to."

He exchanged glances with his wife, who had been listening silently to all this.

"We can't pay out sums like that without knowing whether your films are worth anything or not. In any case, we do not have sums of money like that in the Embassy."

"Then you will have to ask Berlin for them. I shall telephone on October 30, when you will be able to tell me whether or not Berlin accepts my terms."

His wife intervened for the first time. She mentioned a name.

"Moyzisch," she said.

Jenke looked at her thoughtfully, and nodded.

"Yes," he said. "This is a matter for him."

He rose and turned to me.

"It's late," he said slowly. "I'll put you in touch with the

48

right man. It's a matter for him."

I looked at my watch. I had been in the Embassy for three hours already.

I said: "I'm sorry to be taking up so much of your time, but I've been kept waiting here for a long time already. . . ."

Frau Jenke had gone over to the telephone, and she dialled a number. She had to wait a long time before getting a reply.

I did not understand exactly what she said; all I understood was that she insisted that a man named Moyzisch must come to the Embassy immediately.

She put down the receiver, and said to her husband in German: "He was in bed."

"Already?" I said. "It's only half past ten."

The two looked at me.

"So you understand German?"

"Only very little."

Hitherto we had been speaking French.

Jenke said: "I am going to bed too." He did not offer me his hand.

When he reached the door I said loudly: "Will Herr Moyzisch know that I was once your servant?"

Jenke answered coolly: "I can't prevent you from telling him. I had nearly forgotten that you were. The British Ambassador will also one day remember your services with displeasure."

He walked out, and his wife followed him.

Again I had to wait, as I had had to wait so many times that evening. The Germans mistrusted me. The only way of countering this was by patience.

I helped myself to the Jenkes' cigarettes. I found them

less to my liking than the English cigarettes I had got used to at the British Embassy.

Moyzisch was a man of average size, wiry and dark, with alert eyes. He was an Austrian, and his official position at the Embassy was that of Commercial Attaché. In reality he was an *Obersturmbannführer* in the S.S. and worked for Department VI of the *Reichssicherheitshauptamt.** He was responsible, not to von Papen, the Ambassador, but to Ernst Kaltenbrunner, chief of the Department. But all this I found out only later. For the time being I could only assume that he belonged to the German secret service.

Later I read his description of me:

"I guessed that he was in his early fifties," he wrote. "He had thick black hair, brushed straight back from his forehead, which was fairly high. His dark eyes kept darting nervously from me to the door and back again. His chin was firm, his nose small and shapeless. Not an attractive face on the whole. Later, after I had seen a great deal of him, it occurred to me to compare his face to that of a clown without his make-up on—the face of a man accustomed to disguising his true feelings."

That was how I looked to Moyzisch. I felt the contemptuous look in his eyes and his silent astonishment that Herr Jenke had left me alone in his drawing-room.

"Have you been told of my proposition?" I asked.

He shook his head. I remained patient. I was being handed on like a file from one official to the next.

I repeated my story, and he was obviously incredulous. He

---

* Reich Security Department.

found it impossible to believe that I was the British Ambassador's valet. My demand for £20,000 made him smile.

"What is your name?" he asked.

"That is a matter of no importance. Ask Herr Jenke."

"I can't ask Berlin for the money without seeing the film."

"I shall ring you at your office at three P.M. on the 30th. I shall give the name of Pierre."

"So your name is Pierre?"

"The porter at the gate here is named Peter. That gave me the idea, that's all. If you have the money ready when I telephone, we shall meet again."

"Where?"

"There's a tool-shed in the grounds behind the Embassy."

"Oh! You know that?"

"Of course. I shall be there at ten P.M. You can meet me there. You will show me the money, and I will hand the films over to you. You can have them developed on the spot—I assume that you have the necessary facilities at the Embassy."

"Yes."

"You can examine the films while I wait. You need not hand me the money until after you have examined the films and satisfied yourself that they are worth it. That is fair, or isn't it?"

The confidence with which I spoke made him prick up his ears. He started suspecting that perhaps I might be speaking the truth. The incredible began to seem perhaps not so utterly incredible.

"I have something else to put to you," I said quietly. "I need a new camera, a Leica. You will also have to keep me

51

supplied with film. Whenever I hand you exposed film, I want new film from you in return. I don't want to be seen buying film."

He was now listening very attentively indeed.

"Berlin will never agree to pay out the enormous sums of money for which you ask," he said.

"That's your worry, not mine," I said. "I shall be very much obliged if you will now turn off all the lights in the hall and on the staircase. I am going."

He seemed to be wanting to ask many more questions, but I rose to leave. My nerves were at breaking point. The whole thing suddenly seemed to me to be unreal and absurd. I felt hysteria rising within me.

Moyzisch missed his chance. He yielded to my confident manner, and turned off the lights outside. My right hand clutched the rolls of film in my pocket. I clung to them in desperation. If at that moment he had asked me any more questions I should have flung them at his feet, probably with a burst of crazy, hysterical laughter, and I should have felt immense relief if he had taken them for nothing.

Gratefully I disappeared into the darkness of the night.

Next morning this telegram was sent in cipher to Berlin from the German Embassy:

"To the Reich Foreign Minister. Personal. Most secret. We have offer of British Embassy employee, alleged to be British Ambassador's valet, to procure photographs of top secret original documents. For the first delivery on October 30 £20,000 sterling in bank notes are demanded. £15,000 for any further roll of films. Please advise whether offer to be accepted. If so, sum required must be despatched by special courier to arrive here not later than October 30. Alleged valet was employed several years ago by First Secretary, otherwise nothing much known here. Signed, Papen."

The text of this telegram came to my knowledge only ten years later; and the answer, which would have put me into a state of jubilation, also came to my knowledge only when the whole thing was long since over. The answer was as follows:

"To Ambassador von Papen. Personal. Most secret. British valet's offer to be accepted taking every precaution. Special courier arriving Ankara 30th before noon. Expect immediate report after delivery of documents. Signed, Ribbentrop."

While this exchange of telegrams was taking place I was sitting in the Ankara Palace Hotel, drinking, but not getting drunk.

I had crossed the Rubicon, and there was no going back. The tension of waiting for October 30 was almost unbearable, but I must not lose my head.

Moreover, during those few days I had to pay particular attention to my duties as a valet. October 29 was the Turkish national day. On the previous evening there was a diplomatic reception at the Turkish Foreign Ministry. At midday on the day itself President Inönü held a reception for the diplomatic corps, and in the afternoon there was a big military parade on the race-course. It was my responsibility to see that the appropriate dress for each occasion, spotless and perfectly pressed, was punctually laid out for Sir Hughe Knatchbull-Hugessen.

While I was preparing his full-dress uniform for the Presidential reception he walked into the bedroom, looked at me with a smile as I removed one last inevitable speck of dust, and said: "Elyesa, this is the occasion to tell you how very satisfied I am with you. You're an excellent valet."

He said this in his quiet, gentlemanly voice.

"Many thanks, Your Excellency."

I could not bring myself to look at him, but kept my eyes on the uniform.

He was in a very good mood. He went on talking and, though he was more or less talking to himself, this was the first time he had talked confidentially in my presence.

"It is an extraordinary thing being in a neutral country during a war like this," he said. While he spoke I silently handed him the articles of clothing he needed.

"At the military parade your Turkish Government has to take great care to keep the representatives of the hostile Powers well apart. . . ."

"Your Excellency," I said, "if I may say so, I am very glad that my country is neutral."

He looked at me, but ignored the interruption. I knew that in accordance with his Government's policy he was doing everything he could to involve Turkey in the war. He smiled faintly, and went on:

"At the Presidential reception afterwards, the ambassadors are presented in alphabetical order. Do you realise what that means?"

I had been a *kavass* long enough to realise perfectly what it meant.

"They are presented in the French alphabetical order—first Allemagne, then Angleterre, first Germany and then

54

Britain," Sir Hughe Knatchbull-Hugessen continued.

He nodded his head.

"I shall meet the German Ambassador. When Herr von Papen emerges from the audience chamber I shall be waiting outside. We shall greet each other with a barely perceptible bow of the head, without looking at each other. That is the custom. Our peoples are killing each other, and we greet each other."

"That is all very sad, Your Excellency," I said.

He suddenly uttered a dry little laugh, as if he had been struck by a comic idea.

"Years ago, when I was in Peking, Papen's son used to be a friend of the family. We used to get on well."

He laughed again. "How would it be if you popped over to the German Embassy with a little present for Herr von Papen? Something that would give him pleasure?"

My heart stopped still. Had I walked into a trap? Was there some ulterior motive behind Sir Hughe's notable friendliness towards me? Had I been seen entering the German Embassy? The thought made me flush to the roots of my hair. My self-control vanished. My scarlet face at that moment should have been enough to betray me.

But Sir Hughe laughed aloud. "What are you looking so horrified at?" he said. "I just happened to remember that the Turkish national day is also my colleague Papen's birthday. He's sixty-four, if I remember correctly. If it were peace-time, I should naturally congratulate him at the reception. But it's not peace-time, after all. This year he will have to celebrate his birthday without a British present."

I made sure yet again that Sir Hughe's uniform was sitting correctly. I smiled, but it was a very agonised smile.

55

Sir Hughe's little joke had frozen me to the marrow. But then my mood changed. The incident seemed to show that he would never suspect me.

For the first time since leaving the German Embassy I felt I had the strength to reach my goal.

I felt genuinely very sorry for Sir Hughe. He looked very smart when he left the Embassy in the uniform which I looked after for him. As soon as he had gone I hurried to his room with my camera hidden in a duster.

Next day, having been on duty on the Turkish national day, I had the afternoon off.

I met Mara. We strolled down the Atatürk Boulevard, looking at the shop windows. It was a quarter to three. Mara did not know that in a quarter of an hour I was to make the vital telephone call.

"Yesterday I took photographs in the Embassy for the first time," I told her. I had to tell her, to get it off my chest. It was a kind of compulsion. I could not have got through that quarter of an hour without Mara's sustaining admiration.

"In the Embassy?" she exclaimed, as if I had told her something passing human belief.

"Yes, in Sir Hughe's room. I opened the red boxes on his desk and photographed two telegrams."

The sound of my own voice had a calming effect on my nerves.

"I have had duplicate keys made," I went on.

I had had them made by a locksmith, a man who had worked for me many years previously in the Istanbul municipal transport department.

Mara was overcome with retrospective panic on my behalf.

"But suppose the Ambassador had walked into the room," she exclaimed in consternation.

I smiled superciliously.

"He was at President Inönü's reception. I put the telegrams on the window-sill and photographed them."

I looked at my watch. It was five minutes to three. I stopped outside a telephone booth.

I was too agitated to notice a man who was coming towards us, and looked up only when he greeted us.

It was Manoli Filoti, the British Embassy chef. He was much too inquisitive by nature not to want to be introduced to Mara.

"What a lovely day!" he exclaimed. "How are you? Won't you introduce me?"

He preened himself like a peacock and overwhelmed us with a flood of talk, all to make an impression on Mara. He started talking about the Ambassador's favourite dishes and how brilliantly he, Manoli Filoti, cooked them.

Mara and he started eagerly discussing recipes. I heartily wished both of them in hell.

It was three o'clock. I forced my face into a grin. "I have to make a quick telephone call," I said. "Meanwhile you tell Mara how you make *baklava*."

Manoli laughed idiotically, and said to Mara: "Ha—ha—ha! Telephoning another girl while out walking with you!"

I vanished into the telephone booth. There were beads of sweat on my brow. I dialled the number of the German Embassy and asked for Moyzisch. When he answered I gave the code word.

57

"Pierre speaking," I said.

He behaved as if we were old friends. He said he was delighted that we should be able to meet that evening.

I said I was delighted too.

Then he put back the receiver. It was stifling in the booth. I tore open the door and breathed in the fresh air.

So the Germans had accepted.

I was in a fever. I felt that this was the great adventure of my life.

I looked with contempt at that conceited kitchen wizard Manoli. He could not even conceive of such a thing as the £20,000 which was to be mine that evening. I took Mara's arm.

"We must go," I said.

Manoli grinned. He thought I was jealous. I did not care what he thought.

While I was telephoning Moyzisch the Moscow conference of the Allied Powers was just ending. It lasted from October 18 to October 30.

The British Ambassador was duly informed by a Foreign Office telegram of the decisions reached in Moscow. Molotov had insisted that three things were necessary to bring about an early termination of the war. They were: (1) An early invasion of France; (2) increased pressure on Turkey to bring her into the war before the end of the year; (3) pressure on Sweden to enable Allied bases to be established in that country. In regard to point (2), Sir Hughe was instructed to bring the maximum possible pressure to bear on the Turkish Government. He was further informed that on his way back from Moscow Mr. Anthony Eden (as he then was) would be stopping in Cairo, where he wished to meet Mr. Numan Menemencioglu, the Turkish Foreign Minister. The date proposed for this meeting was November 4.

I knew nothing about the end of the Moscow conference, and I had no idea that information about it lay in Sir Hughe's red boxes on the evening of October 30. All I was aware of was the thrill that my luck was still holding.

I laid out the dinner jacket that Sir Hughe was going to wear that evening, and I looked at him with amusement while he put it on. The thought had struck me that next time he went to a diplomatic reception in full-dress uniform I might take advantage of the opportunity to use him to deliver my film. All I would have to do was to pop the film into the pocket of his uniform, from which Herr von Papen could discreetly lift it when the two enemies walked past each other with icy expressions on their faces. This absurd idea caused me a great deal of merriment.

Sir Hughe was in a gay mood too.

"You're looking very pleased with yourself. Did you have a pleasant afternoon?" he asked me.

"Yes, Your Excellency," I replied, truthfully enough.

While he was at dinner I went to his room, opened the boxes, removed the documents from the boxes, closed the boxes again, and hurried to my room. I quickly set up my photographic apparatus, turned on the 100-watt lamp on my bedside table, and photographed the documents.

Less than three minutes later I was back outside Sir Hughe's room with the documents under my jacket. To my horror, the door was ajar. This struck me like a blow. I could hear Sir Hughe's voice. He was telephoning.

If he looked inside the boxes he would find them empty.

I was filled with panic, and for a moment I was rooted to the spot. Then I pulled myself together and walked slowly down the corridor. Behind me I heard the door being quietly closed, and hurried footsteps overtook me. These were those of Sir Hughe on his way back to the family dining-table. He took no notice of me, and there was an expression of annoyance on his face. I knew how he disliked being disturbed by the telephone at dinner.

I walked on slowly until he disappeared.

Then I went to his room and put the documents carefully back in their place.

Two hours later, when I left the Embassy to meet Moyzisch, I did not take the photographs of those documents with me. I was superstitious. That roll of film had nearly brought me disaster. I was not going to risk my neck with it twice in one evening.

The German Embassy grounds were bounded at the back by a wire fence. I knew where there was a hole in it, and I crept through.

I had picked out the tool-shed which was the appointed meeting-place very carefully. It was surrounded by bushes and hidden from view.

I looked cautiously all round, but everything was quiet. I was alone.

It was a cold, clear night. I waited in the shadow of the tool-shed. Moyzisch appeared two minutes early. If he had brought anyone with him, I should promptly have made myself scarce; I trusted him as little as he trusted me. Supposing he had not brought the money? Once more I felt full of doubt. Supposing I were attacked and the film taken from me by force? They would be able to blackmail me into going on working for them—for nothing.

There was no such thing as loyalty and trust in this game.

"Pierre!" he called out softly.

I waited. All was quiet along the pathway behind him. He walked nervously up and down. I stepped forward and said: "Shall we go to your office?"

My sudden appearance right behind his back startled him nearly out of his life.

The building where the Security Department was accommodated was about 120 yards away. We walked there in silence. When we reached the house and started walking down the corridor I noticed that the place was in darkness.

"Your room opens on to the Atatürk Boulevard," I said. "Have you drawn the curtains?"

"You are very well informed," he muttered.

"I have to be."

I knew from the days of my service with Jenke where the office of the secret service people was, though at that time Moyzisch had not been there. He switched on the light in his office and shut the door. We were alone. He had not led me into a trap.

"Show me the film."

We stood facing each other—two men who violently mistrusted each other.

"Show me the money," I replied.

Almost imperceptibly he hesitated. Then he went over to the safe in the corner and opened the steel door, with his back turned to me. Suddenly he turned and looked at me, and I saw a flicker in his eyes. He was afraid of me.

I could not help smiling. His fear caused mine to vanish.

61

"I am unarmed," I said quietly. "This is not a hold-up."

He did not answer. He took a parcel from the safe. The contents were wrapped in a copy of the newspaper *La République*.

I held out the film on the flat of my hand. He could not take his eyes off it while he unwrapped the newspaper. I saw the bundles of money.

He went over to the desk and counted it out while I watched. The total was correct—£20,000.

Now that it lay within my grasp, my greed to lay my hands on it had vanished. The prospect of accepting it seemed to me to be the height of treachery. If there was anything I wanted at that moment, it was not this sum of money which I had long regarded as my own, but more money and still more. Much more.

With rapid movements Moyzisch picked up the money, put it back in the safe, slammed the door, and locked it. "First I must develop the film," he said in a firm voice. "I'm not buying a pig in a poke."

I had no alternative but to give him the film, and he walked quickly out of the room.

I no longer remember what happened inside me during the next quarter of an hour. Did I again fear I was going to be double-crossed? Would they keep both the film and the money and throw me out? Most probably. I just sat there on one of the office chairs, in a daze, waiting in patient apathy for what was going to happen.

It seemed an eternity until he came back. When at last he reappeared in the doorway his face was expressionless. We gazed at each other, weighing each other up. Finally his features relaxed.

"Would you like a glass of whisky?"

"The money first," I replied.

This time he did not hesitate. He handed the small fortune over to me, and he also presented me with a piece of paper.

"Please sign the receipt," he said.

I thought my ears had deceived me, but then I burst out laughing. Laughing got rid of the last trace of my nervousness.

"I'm not such a fool as that," I said.

He looked at the unsigned receipt in his hand, and then grinned.

"We are so bureaucratic," he said, and tore it up.

The whisky was excellent, and we drank each other's health. I emptied my glass in one draught. I wanted to get out of the house as quickly as possible.

I remembered the other things for which I had asked.

"The Leica and the film, please," I said.

He produced them from his desk.

"Anything else?" he asked coolly.

"Yes. Next time I see you I want you to give me a revolver."

"What for?"

"I want a revolver. That is a condition."

"I'll see that you get it."

"Till tomorrow, then," I said, and turned to go.

"Tomorrow?" he asked in astonishment.

"Yes, I shall have some more film for you. I've already . . ."

"I have no money to pay for any more yet," he said uneasily.

63

I shrugged my shoulders. "Then you can pay me later. I'll allow you credit."

I left the German Embassy by the route by which I had come. When I crept through the gap in the fence I was a rich man.

Mara asked no questions about where the money came from. I bought her clothes at the A.B.C. in the Atatürk Boulevard, the smartest store in Ankara.

"If anyone sees us here, they'll wonder how we can afford it," she said.

I made a deprecatory gesture. "They're too stupid to see us," I replied.

I fulfilled Mara's dreams of expensive scent, luxurious underwear—and whisky.

Sometimes I was disgusted at the amount she drank, but I was also fascinated by her lack of inhibitions. Her husky, drunken voice and her fascinating laugh were drugs of which I could not get enough.

We rented a house among the hills of Kavaklidere and stifled our consciences.

"You don't work for the Turkish secret service," she said.

"I never said I did," I said. "That was your own idea."

"I don't want to know where the money comes from."

"I wouldn't tell you in any case."

It was not a big or impressive house, but it was furnished with soft carpets, the refrigerator was always full, and the wireless played perpetual dance music. It was our oasis. Not a single *kavass* in Ankara had a house. The Germans had assigned me a cover-name, *Cicero*; I could not resist pencilling above the door, in tiny letters, the words "Villa Cicero."

One day I caught Mara ransacking the cupboards and drawers. "The money's not here," I said sarcastically.

She did not mind being caught out like this. She was not a bit ashamed of herself. She laughed and embraced me.

We refused to consider the possibility that our recklessness might lead to disaster.

I kept the money in my room in the servants' quarters at the British Embassy. I preferred relying on the unsuspecting British to relying on Mara. I hid the money under the carpet and enjoyed the sensation of treading on it.

My second meeting with Moyzisch was brief. I handed him the film of the Moscow conference documents, and he handed me the revolver.

"You used to be Herr Jenke's servant?" he said.

"If Herr Jenke says so, no doubt that is correct."

"He says that you were his *kavass* six or seven years ago."

If Herr Jenke said that, it was incorrect, however. Six years before he was still in Istanbul. I was his servant in Ankara. Perhaps he was reluctant to admit that I had been an Embassy servant under him as I was now an Embassy servant under Sir Hughe Knatchbull-Hugessen. His brother-in-law Ribbentrop might have been tempted to inquire whether perhaps I had deceived him just as I was now deceiving his British counterpart.

"Herr Jenke must know what he is talking about," I answered Moyzisch.

"He can't remember your name."

"I'm very sorry to hear it," I answered calmly.

"What is your name?"

"When Herr Jenke remembers it, no doubt I shall."

This was one of the many occasions on which Moyzisch tried to get me to disclose my identity.

They gave me this cover-name Cicero because it was the name of a Roman famous for his eloquence. Herr von Papen thought that the documents with which I acquainted him were very eloquent too.

One day Mara found my revolver. "Sometimes you make me very frightened, Elyesa," she said.

"You should call me Cicero," I replied.

She looked at me blankly. Cicero might have meant something to her if it had been the name of a brand of whisky.

"Now there are several people to whom Cicero is the most important man in the world," I told her.

Later I found out that the Germans for a long time doubted the genuineness of my documents. It was inconceivable to the authorities in Berlin that I should have access to such secrets.

However, many years later I read in Papen's memoirs:

"It needed only one glance to tell me that I was looking at a photograph of a telegram from the British Foreign Office to the Ambassador in Ankara. Form, content and phraseology left no doubt that this was the genuine article. It consisted of a series of answers from the Foreign Secretary, Mr. Eden, to questions which Sir Hughe Knatchbull-Hugessen had asked in another telegram requesting guidance on certain aspects of his country's policy, particularly as regards Turkey."

Herr von Papen is referring here to the telegram I photographed while he was meeting his enemy, Sir Hughe

Knatchbull-Hugessen, at the Presidential reception on the Turkish national day.

But Berlin went on believing for a long time that I was trying to practise deception on it. Many months later, when it was all over, it turned out that Berlin had been practising deception on me.

CHAPTER 4

The bank-notes under my carpet multiplied rapidly—£30,-
000, £45,000, £75,000. . . . I had long ceased to count the
wads of notes that Moyzisch handed over to me. I had no
fear of being cheated by the Germans.

Did my character begin to change? I began to attach importance to the care of my hands, and regularly had myself
manicured. After being shaved at the barber's—I had given
up shaving myself—I always had a face massage.

I began to treat Mara with noticeable contempt.

"I hardly ever see you any more," she complained with
an expression of suffering on her face.

"I'm very busy, I've no time," I replied.

"That's not true. You were in the lounge of the Ankara
Palace. I saw you going in."

"Then you know where I was."

A nagging tone came into her voice, which could be so
attractively husky.

So far as I was concerned, she had outlived her useful-
ness. I had no more need to go to the house of Mr. Busk,
the First Secretary; everything I needed was within my
reach in the Embassy. Mara's depression and her consump-
tion of whisky increased.

Portrait of a *kavass* as a gentleman. Cicero took this picture of himself in Herr Jenke's drawing-room

Sir Hughe Knatchbull-Hugessen and Lady Knatchbull-Hugessen

The German Embassy (above) and the British Embassy in Ankara

Planet News Ltd

Franz von Papen (left), German Ambassador in Ankara during the war

L. C. Moyzisch, Cicero's contact at the German Embassy

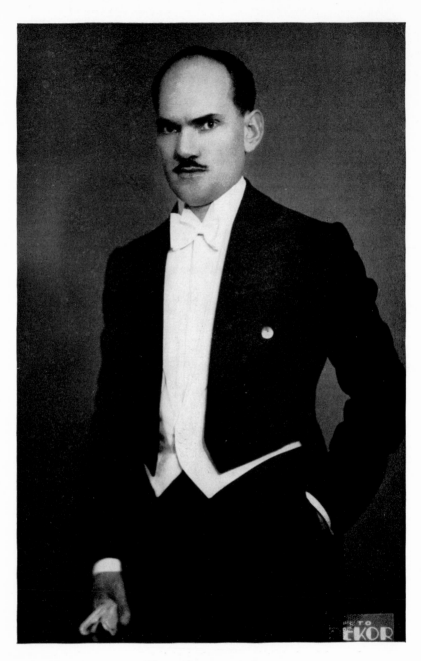

Cicero the concert singer

The Ankara Palace Hotel (left) in which Cicero dreamed of building the Celik Palace Hotel (right)

Cicero today

"You shouldn't drink so much," I told her.

"What business is that of yours?"

I shrugged my shoulders. We now squabbled like cat and dog, and squabbling gave me no pleasure. I kept out of her way.

I sat for hours in my room in the servants' quarters, with my legs sprawling over the yellow carpet, contemplating my filed and polished finger-nails. I had had a new suit made for me by the best tailor in Ankara, but could not risk being seen in it in the Embassy precincts. I used to put it on secretly and admire myself in the mirror—in anticipation of the time of unrestricted lavishness and elegance that sooner or later, perhaps sooner, was to come.

I decided that when the time came I should go to Bursa. Bursa lies at the foot of Mount Uludag, and was founded by Hannibal. It is famous for its hot springs, and is the smartest of the smart. The landscape and the climate resemble those of Switzerland, and it is the pride of Turkey. That is where I would go to take my ease. Nobody would suspect my origin, and I should be a distinguished gentleman among his kind. A retired *kavass*.

It was on one of those evenings in my room that I dreamt for the first time of building a hotel at Bursa.

Meanwhile my impudence grew from day to day. Photographing secret documents in the British Embassy became a form of nervous stimulation for me, a kind of drug that I required to enable me to go quietly to sleep. I played with danger, and for a long time believed it impossible that I should ever be caught.

Mara bombarded me with questions.

"Whom are you working for? Tell me whom you are working for," she insisted.

69

"That's no business of yours."

I bought her expensive dresses and underwear, and reacted to her passionate gratitude with coolness and indifference.

The time of our deep feeling for each other was over. We were carrying our love towards its grave, Mara with tears, I like a distant relative at a funeral he cannot avoid attending.

I kept on photographing everything I could lay my hands on.

Telegram No. 1594 from the Foreign Office, London, to the British Ambassador in Ankara, said:

"You will recall our obligation under the protocol signed in Moscow to bring Turkey into the war before the end of the year."

This telegram was signed by Mr. Eden, the British Foreign Minister, and I hated him for it. Let them get on with their war and finish it, but Turkey must be kept out. Was Bursa to be turned into a battlefield or a bombing target? Bursa, where I was going to build a hotel? What did I care for the world's great men? I would welcome them as guests at the fashionable hotel of which I dreamed, but as the senders of death-bringing telegrams I, a *kavass* playing at destiny, double-crossed them.

Sir Hughe went to see Numan Menemencioglu, the Turkish Foreign Minister. Before he left I handed him a clean handkerchief and his grey gloves. What answer would Numan give the British?

The answer was quoted in Telegram No. 875 from the British Ambassador in Ankara to the Foreign Office in London. It said: "M. Menemencioglu assures me that the Turkish Government will be prepared to take part as soon as it is clear that the allied landings in the west have been successful."

They treated the war like an invitation to a garden party, to which one goes only after making sure that it is not going to rain.

I handed over the film to Moyzisch. We now always met in his car, an Opel Admiral. He drove slowly down a pre-arranged street until he caught sight of me. I would get in quickly, and we would disappear among the winding suburban streets.

I used to crouch in the back seat with my coat collar turned up. We would drive through the Ulus Meydan, the busiest square in Ankara, just one car among innumerable others. It would be hard to follow us. The advertisements flashed and the lights glared through the slight haze of the night.

I stared at the back of Moyzisch's neck. Some day I should have a chauffeur of my own and not have to crouch in the back seat like this.

The streets grew quiet and narrower. I turned and looked through the back window. When I had made sure that nobody was following I sat up and lit a cigarette. This was a sign that the coast was clear. Moyzisch relaxed at the wheel.

I put the photographs I had taken on the seat beside him and took the packet of money that lay there ready for me.

After that he invariably started putting questions to me. He always had a tremendous lot of questions. In that he was just like Mara.

"When did you decide to work for us?"

"Two years ago. I laid my plans well in advance."

I told him whatever came into my head.

"Do you work alone?"

"Yes."

"Berlin refuses to believe that a man can take so many photographs by himself. You must have assistants."

"My hands are my assistants. I have a clever pair of hands."

"It's incredible that secret documents should be left lying about so casually in the British Embassy."

"They are not left lying about casually. Getting at them is a pretty risky business."

I have always enjoyed travelling by car, but I had to pay for it by putting up with his questions. But I did not mind them very much.

"What is your name?"

I forget how many times he asked me that.

I caught his glance in the driving mirror, and grinned.

"Cicero," I replied.

He made an angry gesture and was silent for a time.

"Please put me down somewhere near the British Embassy," I said.

"Isn't that a bit risky?"

"One risk more or less doesn't make much difference."

We turned into the Atatürk Boulevard.

"Why do you work for us?"

"Because you pay well. You know that yourself."

"Is that the only reason?"

"What other reason should I have?"

"I want to know the real reason."

His voice was pressing. He sounded as if he might have understanding for the deepest depths of my soul.

I was silent. Perhaps he was the kind of agent who found it distressing to employ a spy altogether lacking in idealism. The Germans are like that.

He spoke again, quietly and very seriously.

"Tell me the real reason," he said.

I hoisted the flag that he wanted to see flying.

"I hate the British," I said in an expressionless voice.

At last I had given him what he wanted. He nodded, as if I had confirmed something that he had always secretly suspected. For a few moments, out of respect for the greatness of my hatred for the British, he was silent.

I played on his credulity. What I said next burst out of me as if I were confiding to him an intolerably painful memory. The lie that I told him carried me away completely. The thought that it might conceivably have been true made my voice sound hoarse.

"An Englishman killed my father," I said.

Moyzisch started. Now he had what he wanted with a vengeance—a really satisfactory explanation of my espionage activities.

I distracted him from his train of thought.

"I assume you will have no difficulty in having a duplicate key made."

His head was full of the lie I had told him. He fell for it, hook, line and sinker.

"No," he muttered.

I gave him a wax impression of the key of the black box which stood at night on Sir Hughe's bedside table. I said:

"I've had a duplicate key for one of the boxes made myself, but this one is too difficult."

"I'll see to it," he muttered.

73

We drove up the steep street at the end of which the Embassy lay.

"Slow down, please."

He took his foot off the gas.

"I'm very sorry that in the course of asking you questions I mentioned certain matters which . . ."

For a member of the German Security Service he showed great delicacy of feeling.

"Switch off the headlights," I said.

He did so.

I jumped out of the slowly moving vehicle, ran a few steps beside it, and slammed the door. Moyzisch accelerated, and the headlights were switched on again.

I was left standing in the dark street. A shudder went through me. I was filled with fear, fear of my father's anger. My father had died peacefully in his bed, and I had misused his memory. The poplars on the hill stood out like threatening shadows. I grinned sheepishly to try and drive away my fear.

In the light of morning my superstitious ideas vanished, and the light of my 100-watt bedside lamp shone down harshly on documents dealing with the realities of war.

The telegrams and memoranda deciphered for Sir Hughe passed through my room in the servants' quarters. It was a strange kind of nightly colloquy I had with the great ones of the world whose names turned up in the documents: Roosevelt, Hopkins, Churchill, Eden, Stalin, Molotov . . .

Churchill wrote later in his memoirs:

"If we could gain Turkey it would be possible without the

74

subtraction of a single man, ship, or aircraft from the main and decisive battles to dominate the Black Sea with submarines and light naval forces, and to give a right hand to Russia and carry supplies to her armies by a route far less costly, far more swift, and far more abundant than either the Arctic or the Persian Gulf."

That was the problem, succinctly stated. I read it all *in extenso* in the telegrams I photographed. Though sometimes the details were unintelligible to me, at other times the situation was stated with brutal frankness.

The cover-name "Operation Overlord" kept recurring in front of my camera. It gradually dawned on me that this could refer only to the second front that the Russians were demanding of their allies, the second front that was to go into history as the invasion of France.

One telegram said: "If Turkey came in on our side it would free the escort vessels we need so urgently for Overlord."

A memorandum recorded a conversation with the Turkish Foreign Minister. It said that the Turks were hesitating. If only they could be brought in, it would be a dreadful blow to Germany.

The Teheran conference took place from November 28 to December 1, 1943. Stalin announced that when the war was over the German General Staff must be liquidated. The German capacity to commit aggression depended on about 50,000 officers and specialists. "They must be arrested and shot, and then German military strength will be broken for ever."

Churchill said that his greatest worry in connection with Operation Overlord was not so much the landing itself as what might happen a month later, after the Germans had gathered their strength for a counter-stroke. At that moment the Red Army must tie the Germans down on the Eastern front while the Western Powers tied them down in Italy. If the Turks chose that moment to intervene, allied victory was assured.

A telegram to Sir Hughe from the Foreign Office said: "There are seventeen air squadrons in Egypt, sufficient to provide protection if the Turks should feel threatened by German air raids. Also three anti-aircraft regiments could be stationed on Turkish soil."

What Churchill had to say about this was: "What I want is air bases in the region of Smyrna and Badrun. . . . When we get them and put in squadrons we can drive the Germans out of the air. . . . We must starve out the German garrisons on the islands. If Turkey takes an active part the islands will fall of themselves. It would not be necessary in that case to attack even Rhodes. The islands have to be supplied by Germany, and if we have air cover from Turkey our destroyers can cut down German convoys, which they cannot do at present because Germany commands the air. Turkish bases will give us continued pressure against the Germans, and that will be a preparation for 'Overlord.'"

I read all this, photographed it, and jumped into Moyzisch's Opel Admiral for our nightly *rendezvous*, and the Germans knew what their enemies were thinking and planning. Was not Moyzisch one of the 50,000 specialists whom Stalin wanted to have shot?

In my room in the servants' quarters I engaged in imaginary conversations with the world's great men.

What, I said to myself, has Operation Overlord to do with me?

If one single German bomb falls on Ankara and hits me, the *kavass* Elyesa Bazna, what, I said to myself, will be the use to me of your seventeen air squadrons in Egypt?

I knew all about the basement of the British Embassy in Ankara. Perhaps Sir Hughe regarded it as bomb-proof, but I had never met him down there. Personally I regarded the walls as rather weak.

What use will it be to me, I said to myself, if the Germans on the island of Rhodes are starved out and famine comes to Turkey as it does to all countries at war?

I read the documents and, sitting alone in my room, objected violently to the things said in the name of Roosevelt, Churchill and Stalin.

At Teheran Churchill said to Stalin that no effort must be spared to force Turkey into the war. Stalin replied: "I am unconditionally in favour of the attempt. If necessary, we must take them by the scruff of the neck."

I was a mere cipher in this world war, but I was one of the Turks whom Stalin wanted to take by the scruff of the neck. There was nothing I could do to stop him. All I could do was to take my photographs—a mean and shabby little counter-measure, as mean and shabby as the fact that I was taking money for what I was doing.

My daily life was rather like sitting in a cinema and watching a film in which I was not interested. One of the figures on the screen was a British Ambassador who was awakened by his *kavass* with a glass of orange juice at half past seven every morning. The *kavass* wished him good morning and drew the bedroom curtains. Another actor was Lady Knatchbull-Hugessen, the Ambassador's wife, who barely noticed the *kavass's* greeting when she passed him in the corridor. The *kavass* pressed the ambassadorial trousers, ran the ambassadorial bath, and sewed on the ambassadorial buttons.

The *kavass* was I—I distinctly recognised myself in this humble role, which struck me as being so unreal and insignificant.

Were we not all shadows passing without seeing each other? How unreal life was!

I walked down the corridor towards the Ambassador's room. He was out. I had my duster in my hand—the duster that was my passport to the hostile territory in which I carried out sabotage.

Lady Knatchbull-Hugessen passed me. She responded to my greeting with a fleeting nod.

How insignificant I was to Lady Knatchbull-Hugessen! If I were not treated with proper respect, I got my own back. This conceited idea made me smile.

The telephone in Sir Hughe's room was the only one which was not connected to the Embassy switchboard.

I dialled the number of the German Embassy and asked for Moyzisch.

"Pierre speaking," I said. He knew that this meant another appointment. We used to arrange these in a secret agents' jargon which Moyzisch had taught me and I thought absurd.

"What about a game of bridge tomorrow?"

That meant meeting at ten o'clock the same evening at a place decided on at our previous meeting.

78

On this occasion this was obviously inconvenient to Moyzisch. Perhaps there was something else he wanted to do—meet a girl, perhaps, but I did not know.

"Wouldn't later do?" he asked.

"No."

He hesitated. "Can't I get hold of you somewhere else? Can I ring you back?"

I grinned. "Of course," I said. "Ring me back right away. I'm in my chief's room. Do you know the number?"

It took him quite a while to get used to my recklessness.

"You're crackers!" he muttered. "Very well, then, we'll meet for a game of bridge tomorrow."

He put down the receiver as hurriedly as if it were he who was burning his fingers on a British telephone.

I too put down the receiver and carefully dusted the instrument, so that Sir Hughe should have no cause to rebuke his *kavass* for neglecting his duties.

We met at one of the corners of Akay Street in the Kocatepe district. Moyzisch was furious. Because I had spoiled a date he had with a girl? Because of my recklessness? To hell with him.

"You must be out of your mind to call us up on the Ambassador's personal telephone," he said.

"Drive on," I said nonchalantly.

He drove on as if he were working off his indignation on the car.

I said coolly: "It would have been still more reckless to have left the Embassy at that time of the day when it was my duty to be using my duster."

79

"If you had been caught . . ."

"I should have said that I was talking to my girl-friend. If I had told them that I was talking to a German they would never have believed me."

This may have sounded a little far-fetched, but I am convinced that it was true.

"Nothing will happen to me," I said, reclining comfortably in my seat. We exchanged films and money. Moyzisch, still in a bad temper, gave me the duplicate key he had had made for the black box.

"I hope it fits," he muttered.

"I'll try it tonight," I replied calmly.

He glanced at me.

"Sometimes you make me shudder," he said.

I smiled with self-satisfaction. I was delighted at the impression I had made on him.

We drove on through dark, quiet, empty streets. Only occasionally did the lights of another car appear behind us. I opened the window. The cold air did me good.

"Why did the Englishman kill your father?"

His question took me unawares. I pressed my lips together. Why would he persist with his questioning?

"That's nobody's business."

"Berlin wants to know," he said quietly. "They still don't trust you completely."

"That's all the same to me."

For a moment we were dazzled by the headlights of a car behind us. It did not overtake us.

Moyzisch said soothingly: "Now that we know the real reason why you're working for us, Berlin is taking quite a different view. . . ."

"What has my father's death got to do with it? I might have been lying to you."

"I don't believe it," he said earnestly. "Why did the Englishman kill your father?"

He refused to be put off.

"It was apparently a hunting accident," I said. "In the Macedonian mountains. The official inquiries were stopped."

To put a stop to his questioning I said the first thing that came into my head. I begged my father's forgiveness for turning his peaceful death into a lie. Once more superstitious fear got the better of me.

"Do you know the Englishman?"

"Of course! That's enough questions."

"Do you still know him? Is he a diplomatist?" he asked quietly.

What was he driving at? Where was his imagination leading him? Or were these questions dictated by Berlin?

"I'm not answering any more questions."

He grew tense. I noticed how he was gripping the steering wheel.

He drew into the curb and stopped.

"What's the matter?"

He did not answer. Then he drove on again, and turned into the next street. The street was empty, there were no lights in the windows, it was a poor quarter which had cause to be grateful to the night that concealed its wretchedness. The headlights of a car flashed briefly in our driving mirror. Moyzisch was watching the driving mirror. He stepped on the gas, and we drove down the street at speed. I felt the palms of my hands growing moist.

"We're being followed," I exclaimed.

I could tell from the way that Moyzisch was sitting that he was alarmed. He took a corner too fast, the car swayed violently, and he had some difficulty in bringing it under control.

"So you've realised it, have you?" he exclaimed angrily. "Why did you use the Ambassador's telephone, you fool?"

When Moyzisch slowed down the car behind slowed down too. When Moyzisch stopped, the other car stopped. Then a wild pursuit started through the night, but we could not shake off our pursuer.

I had disturbed the peace of a dead man by a senseless lie, and now I was paying for it by this blind fear.

"If it's all up now, it's your own fault!" Moyzisch yelled at me.

I too felt that it was my fault, but not in the way that Moyzisch meant.

"It's not I whom he's after. He didn't start chasing us until long after I got in. It's you who are under observation," I said.

The chase went on, and we squabbled about whose fault it was. We drove at reckless speed down narrow, winding streets. We risked smashing ourselves to bits against a wall, but we went on squabbling.

"Drive towards the Ambassador's quarter," I shouted. "I'll jump out just after you've turned a corner."

Moyzisch did not answer, but drove towards the Cancaya hills.

I clung to the hope that our pursuers knew they were chasing Moyzisch, the German so-called Commercial Attaché, but that they did not know the identity of the man who had got in on Akay Street. It seemed a slender hope. The fear that the game was up was stronger.

"Get ready to jump!"

I was startled by Moyzisch's excited voice. A side-street appeared in front of us in the light of the headlamps, and Moyzisch turned sharply to the right. I pulled myself together. Moyzisch braked so hard that we were nearly lifted out of our seats. I opened the door and flung myself out. I fell, rolled over and over on the pavement, and found myself lying flat on my face in the shadow of a garden fence, panting.

The rear lights of Moyzisch's car disappeared, but before the howl of his engine had faded away the other car appeared and dashed past me.

There was only one occupant, a shadow crouching over the steering wheel. For a fraction of a second I thought I saw a face in the faint light of the instrument panel. Did I only imagine that it was a young, smooth, expressionless face?

It took me quite a time to become aware of the sudden silence. Somewhere the chase was still going on in the night, but I was alone.

Did I imagine that I should never forget that young, smooth face and would be able to pick it out again among a thousand?

I lay on my bed fully clothed and utterly exhausted. Thoughts hammered in my head. Why could I not stop thinking?

Did they suspect me? Did the man with the young, smooth face know whom he was chasing? Did Sir Hughe know what I was doing? If so, how had he found out? Why had I returned to the Embassy? Wouldn't it have been better to go away and hide? But supposing they still suspected nothing?

I found no answers to my questions, but I could not shake them off. I had to find some way of coping with my fear.

I was clutching the duplicate key of the black box. For a moment I was tempted to fling it out of the window. But I knew I should never do it. The compulsion to try it was stronger.

But why the compulsion? I could find no explanation. Did I need victory over my fear that night in order to be able to shout in their faces next morning that I was the man whom they were after?

I rose stiffly to my feet. My limbs felt paralysed. I made my camera ready and put the 100-watt bulb in the lamp. I did all this with slow, mechanical movements. The manual dexterity of which I was so proud had vanished.

I walked out into the passage. All was quiet. In my stockinged feet I passed the painting of King George VI.

I had no alternative to doing what I did, it would have been impossible for me to act differently. My fear remained. It would have been a relief if they had caught me at that moment. Outside the Ambassador's bedroom I did not hesitate. I moved slowly, as if in a trance, but I did not hesitate.

Noiselessly I opened the door, closed it behind me, and went over towards the bed. I did not stop at the door, and I did not stop to listen to the Ambassador's breathing. I went straight over to his bed, and did not stop until I got to the night table on which the black box lay.

I had walked into the lion's den. The Ambassador might have opened his eyes and he might have been staring at my shadow, which was darker than the darkness of the room. I dared not look in his direction. If I had, I should have let out a hysterical yell.

A narrow strip of weak light lay across the black box. Perhaps the curtain was not drawn properly. I did not look to see.

I put the key in the lock and turned it. Softly I opened the box, fumbled for the papers, and removed them. Next to the box there was a glass of water. It was empty. The Ambassador had taken his sleeping pills as usual. But perhaps he was only trying to trap me. I was incapable of thinking any thought to the end.

I turned and left the room.

Back in my own room, I gazed at the papers, and suddenly my hands began to tremble. I lay on the bed and waited for the trembling to stop.

Had the Ambassador really been in his bed? Or was the bed by any chance still untouched? I should have been unable to say.

I got up and photographed the documents. I was incapable of taking in the meaning of the words. Only one phrase in one document penetrated to my consciousness. I recognised Sir Hughe's handwriting; it was a telegram he had drafted himself. It would be put into cipher tomorrow morning before being sent off to the Foreign Office in London.

The words that I read were: "Papen knows more than is good for him."

I dismantled my apparatus and hid it, as well as the camera and the film.

So they knew that Papen knew. . . . But did they know from where he got his knowledge?

I switched off my bedside lamp and took the papers back to the Ambassador's bedroom. Suddenly I was clear-headed and as cold as ice. They knew. . . .

I opened the door and listened. I heard the breathing of a sleeping man. The strip of light that came in through the curtain fell right across the bed. I saw a pale, slack face. I went over to the bedside table.

I gazed at Sir Hughe. My face twisted into a mocking smile. Whatever the sleeping man knew, he knew nothing about me.

I put the papers back in the box—and then it happened. In removing the key from the lock I upset the tumbler, which smashed to pieces on the floor.

I froze, and held my breath. The extraordinary thing was that I felt no fear. There was no trace of fear or rage or terror in me. I bent over and looked into the face of the sleeping man.

He stirred, and lay still again. My staring eyes gazed at his, which were closed. He breathed heavily, as if he had a cushion over his face. I gazed at him, and felt that he was dreaming that a threat hung over him.

CHAPTER 5

I suspected Mara. Why should she not have given me away? The arrogance and contempt with which I had treated her recently must have made it clear to her how little I had come to care for her.

We were sitting in the little house that I had rented.

There were pot-plants in every corner, and we had a blind canary; the dealer had told us that canaries sang the better for being blinded. There was also a hookah, which I did not smoke, bought for me by Mara with my money. The wireless was on, the canary chirped, the hookah grew dustier and dustier, and the whisky bottle was always within reach. Such was domestic bliss as understood by Mara.

I scrutinised her, looking for some sign that she had betrayed me.

Had she betrayed me to Mr. Busk the First Secretary at the Embassy? Perhaps she had not told him the whole story, but just given him a hint. "Mr. Busk, I know something, not details, of course, but . . ."

Perhaps all that she had had in mind was a minor act of feminine vengeance, but for me it could have the gravest consequences.

"How's the Busk baby?" I asked, as if I were greatly interested in the infant's health.

Her answer was monosyllabic. "Well," she said.

Mara had changed. Normally she talked to me endlessly about the child.

She was aware of my nervous state. She looked at me with a strange expression in her eyes. Or did I only imagine it?

I told myself that I was seeing ghosts. But there was no defence against them.

"Are you having any trouble with the Ambassador?" she asked.

The question took me aback. I looked at her, trying to divine what was going on in her mind.

"No," I answered. "Why should I?"

Why had she asked that question? What did she know?

"I was only thinking. You're so strange nowadays," she said.

She did not look at me as she said this. Her voice sounded perfectly normal. She was busy polishing her finger-nails.

Once I had admired the delicacy of her hands. Now I thought them bony. Her legs were skinny, her blue eyes empty and expressionless, and her husky voice had lost its magic for me. It now seemed simply the result of too many cigarettes and still more alcohol. She had lost her attraction for me and I now looked at her with different eyes.

"I'm not strange," I muttered angrily.

I was not having any trouble with the Ambassador. On the morning after that dreadful night I had gone to his bedroom as usual. As usual, I had drawn the curtains, wished him good morning, and offered him his orange juice. Everything was perfectly normal.

The broken glass I had upset during the night lay beside the bed. If I had removed it during the night he would have realised that someone had been in the room.

He sipped his orange juice as usual. When he put down the glass he noticed the broken fragments on the floor.

I felt myself growing tense.

He frowned, as if he were trying to remember something.

"I must have upset it in my sleep," he muttered.

I pretended only just to have noticed the broken glass. Hastily I bent down and started picking up the pieces.

"Mind you don't cut your fingers," he said, and picked up the morning papers I had brought him.

His behaviour towards me was perfectly normal all day. But I knew that during the day he sent off to London the telegram I had photographed the night before. The telegram saying: "Papen knows more than is good for him."

Why did he show no sign?

He must have wondered where Papen got his information from. He must have felt worried or nervous or mistrustful about the people by whom he was surrounded. If he had asked me questions trying to trip me, if he had shown the slightest sign of the suspicion that he must have felt about me, it would have seemed more natural than this perfectly normal behaviour of his.

He was a diplomatist, and all his life he had been forced to control his impulses, and he had learnt to remain invariably cool and polite, at garden parties, declarations of war, and changes of government. Perhaps the long, tedious years of diplomacy had long since made him incapable of being really afraid, or really mistrustful, or of realising the difference between a diplomatic protest and a real earthquake.

His imperturbability nearly drove me out of my mind.

The appalling state of uncertainty I was in made me irritable and bad tempered, and I vented my feelings on Mara. I could not stand the smug way in which she was sitting around.

"Aren't you ever going to finish polishing your nails?" I burst out.

She spread her fingers and breathed on her nails to dry them. She was very cool and self-possessed.

"I should like to know what on earth has come over you," she said with a pout. She shifted in her chair. She was being kittenish. It got on my nerves.

I tried to regain my self-control. After all, nothing had happened. Everything was going on perfectly normally.

I had rung up Moyzisch.

"Pierre speaking," I said, as usual. We met this time in a street among the hills. We noticed a strange motor-car in the distance, but the coast was clear.

I got into the Opel.

"How did you get home?" I asked Moyzisch.

He shrugged his shoulders, and looked mistrustfully all round for the pursuer of yesterday who had not turned up today.

"He vanished," he replied. "I suddenly noticed he wasn't behind me any more."

What could be the explanation of that? Had the man noticed that I was no longer in the car, and was that why he had given up the chase? That would mean that he knew to whom the car belonged and who the driver was, and that all he was interested in was the passenger, that is to say, me. In other words, he wanted to find out who I was, and this time he had failed. So my identity was still unknown to the man on my trail. In other words, nothing had happened.

I gave Moyzisch the film that I had exposed during the night.

"I went into the Ambassador's bedroom," I said quietly. To impress Moyzisch I suppressed all trace of nervousness. "It was quite easy, he had taken his sleeping pills as usual."

Moyzisch looked at me.

"What?" he exclaimed. "You took photographs last night?"

"Why not?"

He said no more.

"What reason have the British to believe that there's a spy in the Embassy working for the Germans?" I asked.

Moyzisch connected my question with last night's chase.

"You may be right," he said. "Perhaps they don't suspect anything. Perhaps last night's chase was just an accident. The man may have been drinking, and he may have chased us just for the fun of the thing. How should I know? Perhaps I was just being subjected to a routine observation. I don't believe the enemy really believes me to be a commercial attaché."

"I'm not referring to the chase," I said. "I'm referring to a passage in the documents that you will be able to read when you have developed the film."

I told Moyzisch about the British Ambassador's remark that Papen knew more than was good for him.

He could not tell me what had put the British on the alert. He could find no possible explanation to drive away the ghosts that had started haunting me.

Many years later I found the explanation in the memoirs of Franz von Papen, the German Ambassador. I read how, armed with the knowledge that he had got from me, he went to see Numan Menemencioglu, the Turkish Foreign Minister. Papen, of course, was a diplomatist and a politician; he had an overall view of events, and obviously he had to do something. Obviously he had to fire a warning shot across the Turkish bows to dissuade them from finally committing themselves to the British side. I, a mere venal spy, was of course told nothing about this. I was too disreputable to be involved in great affairs of state; and was not the danger to which I was exposed a matter of indifference to Papen? What he wrote was this:

"A number of the British telegrams made it seem advisable to intervene immediately with Numan. I need only mention the telegram announcing the proposal to set up radar stations in European Thrace to enable the British bombers to bomb the Rumanian oil-wells still more accurately. This seemed to me to call for an immediate protest. I must therefore give Numan to understand that in one way or another I had obtained knowledge of the British plans for this. I told him that the British Air Attaché or his colleague had mentioned such plans to representatives of neutral Powers; it was my duty to draw his attention to the grave dangers that would arise if the presence of such radar stations came to the knowledge of Berlin. In such an eventuality it would hardly be possible for me to prevent a German reprisal raid on Istanbul. Numan was very astonished at the extent of my knowledge, and in his consternation at what I told him he passed it on to the British Ambassador. Next day a telegram lay on my desk which Sir Hughe sent to the Foreign Office about this. 'Papen knows more than is good for him.'"

So it was Papen himself who put the sleeping British on the alert.

But at the time, when it would have been really important to have known this, I was of course completely in the dark. I did not know what Papen had done. All I was aware of was my fear which I could not drive away.

I made Moyzisch put me down near my little house. There I found Mara, lounging in an easy chair, busy with her finger-nails, surrounded by canary, hookah, pot-plants and whisky bottles. An idyllic scene. It made my blood boil.

I tried to relieve my feelings by upsetting Mara. "I've just had a letter from a relative," I told her.

"So what?"

She was not interested, and went on fiddling with her nails, keeping time with the music on the wireless. The tune they were playing was *La vie en rose*, the latest thing from France.

That morning I had had a letter from Mehmet, a distant cousin.

"My dear Elyesa, we all hope you are well," he wrote. Letters from relatives who have not written to you for ages but now want something from you invariably begin like that.

"Do you remember our little Esra?" Mehmet went on.

93

"She has done very well, and we are very pleased with her. Her school reports were excellent. . . ."

There was a lot more about little Esra, whom I could not remember. When I last saw him, Cousin Mehmet had had a large number of small daughters swarming about.

"Do you think you could do anything for Esra in Ankara? We should be tremendously grateful to you. She is well educated and went to a commercial college."

I had put the letter aside without thinking any more about it. I have never had much use for relatives. Cousin Mehmet seemed to think that, because I worked at the British Embassy, I was capable of performing miracles.

I looked at Mara with a malicious grin.

"We shall have to make a room free," I said. "I shall have to let Esra live here."

I had suddenly remembered Cousin Mehmet's letter, and what I said put Mara on the *qui vive*.

"Who is Esra?" she asked sharply and venomously.

I grinned.

"A relative. I've hardly ever seen her. She has finished with school now, and . . ."

"She's not coming to live here!"

Mara spoke as if the house belonged to her.

"I've got to help her," I murmured gently. "She's the daughter of a cousin to whom I owe a great deal."

In fact I owed Mehmet nothing.

"What does she want here? Why is he sending her here?"

"Heavens, how should I know? Ankara is the capital of Turkey, and the girl wants to get on in the world. I have connections, and I can help her."

Mentioning Esra worked like a charm. I had made Mara

94

jealous, and she boiled with rage. Then she grew gentle and affectionate, and tried to persuade me that Esra would be a disturbing element in our little love-nest.

She kissed me, but my temperature remained below zero. I listened to Mara's declarations of affection as if I had cotton-wool in my ears.

But what she said rang true. Her feelings for me were still alive. It could not have been she who had betrayed me.

I breathed more freely. My confidence and sense of superiority returned, combined with a feeling of sympathy for Mara. I regarded her as a stranger, and I could be fond of her as I had never been fond of anybody before, but it was a superficial fondness, something of the kind that one feels momentarily when one pats a captive animal affectionately on the snout in the zoo, only to forget it immediately afterwards.

Mara lay still in my arms.

Again she quietly said something that took me aback.

"Esra will not come and live here. You're working for the Germans. Now I know—and that's why she won't come and live here."

One of the ghosts that I feared had put on flesh and blood. Mara was threatening me.

I smacked her face, hard.

Mara had happened to overhear a conversation between Mr. and Mrs. Busk. The First Secretary, like all the other Embassy officials, was worried. He had told Mrs. Busk that the Germans must have an excellent source of information, perhaps actually inside the Ambassador's residence.

Mara had overheard this, and to her it was obvious who the excellent source of information was.

I dragged this information from her bit by bit.

"I happened to overhear it by pure chance, and I swear to you that's all I know. It's really all I know," she said.

I did not know whether or not to believe her. But, even if she were lying, she stuck to her story.

She swore that she loved me and had no intention of threatening or blackmailing me, and that she had told me everything she knew.

I tormented her with my mistrust, but succeeded neither in banishing my fear nor in convicting her of being the enemy whom I feared her to be. The truth was as obscure as ever.

When I went to work at the Embassy next morning I noticed a tall, slender man on the opposite side of the street, facing the entrance. He lit a cigarette, sheltering the match in the hollow of his hand. Was he trying to hide his face? Was he watching me? He had a young, smooth face. It was the face of my pursuer.

I was overcome with panic, in the power of which I lay bound and gagged.

I could feel myself slowly losing my grip, and all my efforts to regain self-control were in vain.

I rolled back the carpet in my little room. The money was still there, spread out on the floor like another carpet, the most valuable carpet imaginable. I picked up the bank-notes, and rubbed them between my fingers as if I could not believe my eyes.

Sometimes I thought how reckless it was to leave the money under the carpet in my room like this. I had con-

sidered using an alternative hiding-place under the basement steps, where there was a loose stone, but my pride, as
well as the thought that somebody else might find it just
as accidentally as I had, prevented me. Also there was
the pleasure I took in gloating over my treasure every
evening in my room.

I now started gathering up the bank-notes to take them
down to the basement, but again I hesitated, and ended by
leaving them where they were.

I cursed my inability to make up my mind. I also cursed
my fear, for which I could find no real justification.

I went from one extreme to the other. Outwardly I took
pains to appear completely relaxed and calm, as if I secretly
hoped to banish my fear that way.

In the kitchen I ran into Manoli Filoti.

I forced my face into a grin.

"What do you say of a father who wants to entrust his
daughter to me?" I said.

Manoli had a chicken in the pot.

"How old is the girl?"

"She must be about seventeen."

"Then her father must be a perfect fool," Manoli said
with a grin.

Mustafa said: "Get her a job as lady's maid to Lady
Knatchbull-Hugessen, and then we'll all be able to have a
go at her."

"That would suit you nicely, wouldn't it?" I said.

Manoli stroked the chicken's leg as appreciatively as if it
had been a girl's.

"Not at all a bad idea," he said with a grin. "As I go
home every evening, she could sleep in my room."

97

"And some evenings, no doubt, you wouldn't go home," I said.

We went on making the usual below-stairs jokes. I laughed the loudest.

"Is your Esra attractive?" Manoli asked.

"At seventeen she could hardly be anything else," I answered. "I'll have a word with Lady Knatchbull-Hugessen."

It had struck me that it might be quite an idea to get Esra a job in the Embassy. I might be able to use her as my assistant.

"She might be useful to all of us," I said with a grin, and Manoli and Mustafa grinned too.

Esra had suddenly become very important to me, and she became associated in my mind with the idea that the threatening shadows existed only in my imagination, and that there was no reason why I should not go on with what I was doing. If I did something positive, I should cease to be afraid. At any rate, that was what I tried to persuade myself.

I went to see Lady Knatchbull-Hugessen.

I told her that a girl relative of mine was coming to Ankara, and that I had nowhere to put her up. Did Lady Knatchbull-Hugessen by any chance require . . .

She listened to me coolly. No, she said, she did not want another maid, but the girl could stay at the Embassy for a few days until she found something. She said all this with friendly indifference.

"I am very grateful to you, madam," I said, and left the room with a bow.

I refused to admit to myself that while talking to Lady

Knatchbull-Hugessen I had scrutinised her closely. I refused to admit to myself that my only purpose had been to see how the Ambassador's wife would react to my request. If there had been the slightest suspicion of me in her mind, would she not have rejected it out of hand?

But no, obviously she suspected nothing. Nobody knew that Cicero was I. I felt triumphant, and my courage returned.

That day I was completely out of my senses.

After lunch the Ambassador used to play the piano in the drawing-room. That day he rang and asked for a glass of fruit juice, and I took it to him. I listened respectfully to the music.

"Your Excellency plays very well indeed," I said.

"Many thanks," he said with a smile.

I rolled my eyes and laid my hand on my heart in an attitude of musical ecstasy.

I burst into song—the song in which the Flying Dutchman makes his entry.

"Once more seven years are o'er and I am cast contemptuously ashore. Ha! proud ocean . . ."

As I said, that day I was completely out of my senses. I stopped short in the middle of a phrase and assumed a guilty expression.

"Pardon me, Your Excellency," I said.

Sir Hughe laughed, and nodded his head.

"Your voice is not at all bad. It sounds as if you've had some training."

"I have had some training, Your Excellency. I attended the Conservatoire at Istanbul."

Was I mad or was he?

99

He struck a few notes on the piano, and smiled. I recognised the tune. I laid one hand on the piano, and sang:

"In einem Bächlein helle, da schoss in froher Eil
die launische Forelle vorüber wie ein Pfeil . . ."

The Ambassador accompanied me admirably; he led my voice with true artistry.

No, he would never suspect me, never. We made music together far too melodiously for that.

"Ich stand an dem dem Gestade und sah in süsser Ruh'
das muntern Fischleins Bade in klaren Wasser zu."

We were carried away by the music. The room was filled with harmony. Two admirers of German *Lieder* had found their way to each other.

"Doch plötzlich war das Wasser trübe,
und eh' ich mich's versah . . ."

We finished the song. Each of us modestly pooh-poohed the compliments showered on him by the other. The wonderful thing about music is its soothing effect. In any case, when I reverted from the role of singer to that of servant and withdrew with the Ambassador's empty glass, I decided that I had no reason whatever to be afraid of him.

He went on playing for more than an hour. The music re-echoed through the house, and I used the time to photograph some documents. One of them mentioned that on January 14, 1944, there was to be a heavy allied air raid on Sofia. I thought of the reception that the Germans would prepare for the bombers.

After emerging from my room in the servants' quarters I met Mara. The Ambassador was still playing the piano.

She was standing at the staff entrance, and she had the Busks' baby with her in the pram.

I looked hard at her. She had never been here before. I walked slowly over towards her.

She bent over the baby.

"This is where your daddy works," she said to it. It was the kind of senseless remark that people make to babies.

She remained bending over the baby, and looked up at me. I forced myself to smile and take an interest in the baby. I wagged two fingers at it. "What a big girl you're getting!" I exclaimed.

"Isn't she?" said Mara, as if she were the mother, and she gave a rather forced laugh.

Then she said something else, so quietly and in such a strained voice that I only just made it out.

She said that she had heard Mr. Busk telling his wife that some security men had just arrived from London.

Aloud she said: "Which is Mr. Busk's window?"

"He works next door," I answered.

I tickled the baby's cheek, and looked at Mara as she walked away slowly behind the pram.

I had thought her capable of betraying me, but instead she had given me a warning.

I had lost count of time since beginning to play my dangerous game. Then it had been autumn, and now winter was here, and I had taken no notice of the fleeting weeks. For me one day was just like another. All that I lived for was the daily thrill. Now they had sung their Christmas carols at the British Embassy, and I had seen the Christmas tree in the German Embassy, but what did I care? For me nothing existed but my obsessional greed for money, my compulsive craving for the daily thrill—and my fear.

Now I realised that, in my confidence that I should never be found out, I had been putting my head in the noose daily for three months.

It was January. A well-wrapped-up baby with red, frosty cheeks had reminded me of the passage of time; and time must surely be on the side of those who were on my trail.

I hurried back to my room, collected the money, the films, and the photographic apparatus, tucked them under one of the Ambassador's jackets on which I had sewn some buttons, and hid all the incriminating material under the stairs. If it were found there I should be no more suspect than anyone else in the house.

Now nothing was left under the carpet in my room. Now there was no money there for me to see or tread on, and for the first time I had the feeling that what I was doing was completely idle and useless.

Mara had warned me just in time.

When Sir Hughe rang for me and I went to his room, two men were sitting with him. When I walked in they looked at me appraisingly. They scrutinised me with professional mistrust. A third man who had been kneeling in the corner rose to his feet. There was a concealed safe there. Had he been examining it?

"Please bring us some coffee," Sir Hughe said. His tone was as friendly as usual. Suddenly it seemed to me to be impossible that only an hour previously I had been singing to his accompaniment. Had the three agents only just arrived, or had they been in the house for some time? Had Sir Hughe perhaps just taken advantage of an amusing opportunity and kept me singing in his room to enable my room to be searched at leisure? He was just as entitled to use his wits as I was.

I brought them coffee. While I handed round the cups they all seemed to be looking at me searchingly.

"How long have you been with me now, Elyesa?" Sir Hughe asked.

"Three months, Your Excellency."

He spoke to me in French. To the others he said in English: "I'm very satisfied with him."

They made no comment on the Ambassador's remark.

One of them said to me in English: "Bring me some more milk, please."

"Yes, sir," I answered.

"And some sugar," he added casually, in German.

I was just going to let him see that I had understood when I realised that this was a trap.

I said quietly in French: "I beg your pardon, sir, I hardly understand German."

I looked Sir Hughe straight in the eye, and added: "I only know the words of a few German *Lieder* by heart without understanding them properly."

Sir Hughe returned my gaze. The ordeal ended in my favour.

"Some more sugar for the gentleman," he said in French. He seemed to disapprove of these secret service methods; he had too much delicacy of feeling for this world.

I fetched the milk and the sugar, though they had

plenty already. I found it hard to prevent my hands from trembling.

I made an appointment with Moyzisch.

It took quite a time to get through. He seemed to have a new secretary.

"Pierre speaking. Can I speak to Herr Moyzisch, please?"

The secretary hesitated for a moment, and said:

"Whom do you want to speak to?"

"Herr Moyzisch. Tell him that Pierre wants to speak to him."

She had a pleasant, gentle, clear voice, but seemed a little slow on the uptake. She laughed.

"Pierre?" she said. "Pierre what?"

She seemed to be ready for a mild flirtation with the unknown caller, but I was in no mood for it.

"Just Pierre," I said. "Put me through, please."

"Very well," she said coldly.

Her voice really sounded very agreeable, and I was sorry I had been abrupt with her. "I'm sorry, but I'm not in form today," I muttered, but then I heard Moyzisch's voice, and we arranged to meet.

We drove through suburban streets, as usual.

"They've put their agents on the trail," I told Moyzisch, who listened very attentively to what I told him.

"Are you sure?"

"Yes. They've been sent specially from London."

"Then things are going to get tough. Do you want to lay off for a bit?"

I shrugged my shoulders. "I shall have to wait and see. They've searched all the servants' rooms."

"Not just yours, then?"

"I can't say for certain whether they've searched my room or not. But Mustafa has complained that someone has been at his things. They certainly left no trace in my room."

"In that case they have no definite suspicions yet."

"They haven't found the camera or the money. They are well hidden."

We exchanged films and money, and wondered whether this was the last time.

"One of them examined the concealed safe in Sir Hughe's room," I said.

Moyzisch looked at me.

"In that case they don't even know how their secrets have been got at," he said with a reassuring smile.

"Why do you say that?"

"Because they're obviously looking for hidden microphones. If they examined the safe, they must suspect hidden microphones. They don't realise that what they ought to be looking for is photographic apparatus."

His certainty about this filled me with relief. My nerves were so tense that I was ready to clutch at any straw.

I laughed hectically. "I'm not worrying," I said. "But both Sir Hughe and I are a bit nervous. Each of us for different reasons, of course. But today we started making music together, and that gives us both the strength to go on."

Moyzisch looked at me as if he doubted I were in my right mind.

His amazement flattered me, and I grinned.

"I sing, and he accompanies me on the piano," I ex-

plained. "If these fellows had discovered a concealed micro-
phone, their ears would have dropped off in surprise when
they played back the recording."

This idea put us in a good mood.

When we parted, I said: "Please apologise for me to
your secretary. I was rather abrupt with her. She's a new
girl, isn't she?"

"Yes. She has just come from Sofia."

"Well, she's very lucky. She got out of it just in time."

"Why?"

"Have a look at the film. There's going to be a heavy
raid on Sofia in a week's time."

I got out and went to see Mara, to thank her for the
warning she had given me.

I had been afraid of ghosts; of Mara, whom I had suspected of giving me away; of the smooth-faced, unknown
young man I had believed to be on my trail; of security
agents, who were looking for hidden microphones instead
of for my Leica.

I thought I had driven the ghosts away. No sign, no
instinct, warned me that that day I had spoken to my real
enemy—the woman who was to find me out, the woman
who was on the trail of the man whose identity was concealed behind the name of Cicero.

I had been afraid of ghosts and shadows. What I should
have been afraid of was a voice, the bright, pleasant voice
of Moyzisch's new secretary.

Since that time I have thought a lot about that girl:
thought about her, speculated about her and hated her. I
learnt something about her, and had my only sight of her,

while our duel of wits was still going on, but it was not until I came to write this book that I was able to fill in the details. With the help of Herr Nogly and of two clever German journalists I was at last able to satisfy my curiosity about the enemy whom I had first heard speaking on Moyzisch's telephone: about Cornelia Kapp.

I had supposed that the British were on my tracks, but Cornelia Kapp, Moyzisch's new secretary, the pretty twenty-three-year-old blonde daughter of a German diplomatist, was working for the Americans. I have read what she herself was to say about her career: "I was six when I first visited the United States," she wrote. "I was born in Berlin, but I was never really at home in Germany. My father was consul in Bombay before he was transferred to the United States. He became Consul-General at Cleveland, Ohio. I made all my friends in the United States, and I remained in Cleveland until the war broke out. I returned to Germany with my family in 1941."

Her father served in Italy, and then in Bulgaria.

"I received a few weeks' training as a nurse in Stuttgart. I did this reluctantly, but had no choice. Otherwise I should have had to work in a factory. Thanks to my father's connections, I was able to leave Stuttgart and join him in Italy. In July, 1943, I accompanied my parents to Sofia, where my father was appointed to the German diplomatic mission. I worked as a secretary in the German Embassy. It was no accident that I went to Ankara. Through its contacts in Ankara the American secret service got in touch with me in Sofia in August, 1943, and I engaged in espionage work for the Americans in Sofia. In Ankara Moyzisch made my work for the Americans easy. After only four days I had a key to his safe and copied out secret documents. My brothers Peter and Torard were officers in the German Army and were fighting on the Russian front—that was another thing that made it easy for me to gain Moyzisch's confidence. He fell for all my play-acting. A young love affair dating from my Cleveland days played a big part in making me willing to work for the American secret service. I shall not mention the name of the man concerned; I met him again in Ankara when he was an agent of the American O.S.S., the Office of Strategic Services."

In Sofia she had talked her father into finding her a job in a neutral country, Turkey for instance, where life would be more attractive for a young woman. It was by pure chance that she went straight to the source and fountainhead, to Moyzisch himself, who happened at that moment to be requiring additional staff. She would have accepted any job in the German Embassy.

She was her father's favourite, and believed herself to have been favoured by destiny because she had met her young love again, and she was ready to pay any price for this.

She sat in Moyzisch's ante-room, fair, innocent, industrious. When the telephone rang, she lifted the receiver.

"Commercial attaché's office," she said.

I was struck by her bright, pleasant voice.

"Pierre speaking. Herr Moyzisch, please."

I attributed her hesitation and her questions to the fact that she was new in the office.

"Pierre? Pierre what?"

She laughed, and delayed putting me through to

Moyzisch as long as she could—and I thought she wanted a brief flirtation on the telephone.

But she realised she was talking to Cicero.

"I worked exclusively for the American secret service," Cornelia has written. "Moyzisch never knew what I was doing. I knew about Cicero before it became my task to open the mail that arrived in the German Embassy every evening by courier from Berlin. As I worked alone and undisturbed, I had plenty of time to copy out documents from Berlin which made it clear that Cicero was to be sought in the British Embassy itself. I handed over the copies to the Americans every evening. The Americans once nearly caught sight of the man who used often to meet Moyzisch in the evening and always jumped into his car. That was on the evening when Moyzisch and Cicero only just managed to get away after a wild car chase through the whole of Ankara. The Americans had known for some time that a man known as Cicero really existed in flesh and blood. It was my task to establish his identity."

How was Cornelia able to say that she already knew that Cicero existed? Where did she get that information from? How and from whom did she get that knowledge?

The reputation that gathered round the name of Cicero was flattering to my vanity. The name was bandied about in the German Foreign Ministry and at German security headquarters. It was talked about both at Hitler's headquarters and in the office of Allen Dulles, the head of the American secret service and brother of John Foster Dulles, who subsequently became American Secretary of State.

Gossip about Cicero flourished among agents and diplomatists on both sides.

"Cicero? Why, he's a British agent, they use him to lead the Germans up the garden path."

"Cicero is the boy-friend of a British homosexual diplomatist. It's easy enough for him to get at secret documents!"

"Cicero does not exist. He's just an invention of the German propaganda machine."

One night when I went to Moyzisch's office Herr Jenke turned up.

"If things ever get too hot for you in your dangerous work, just come to us," he said. "We'll send you to Germany. The Führer has ordered that after the war you are to be given a villa as a reward."

"You have talked to Hitler about me?"

"Of course!"

I, a mere *kavass*, preened myself.

Franz von Papen says in his memoirs, in the course of an account of a conversation with Hitler: "In my remarks about the general situation I mentioned knowledge about the Teheran decisions made available to us by Cicero's telegrams."

Moyzisch, in an account of an interview with the German Foreign Minister, says: "Ribbentrop still did not deign to look at me. His hands were toying nervously with the documents in front of him. Uncertainty and annoyance were clearly legible on his face as he glanced at the pile of glossy documents that had so far cost the Reich £65,000. With a sudden gesture he thrust the whole batch away from him, over to the far side of his desk. Almost inaudibly his lips formed the words: 'Too good to be true.' "

Moyzisch also quotes Kaltenbrunner as having said: "Ribbentrop is still firmly convinced that the British sent the valet to you and that the whole thing is a plant. I know Ribbentrop. You can be quite sure that he will stick to that theory out of sheer pig-headedness. At any rate it will take him a long time to change his mind. Meanwhile intelligence of incredible importance is simply rotting in his desk and being wasted. We can't afford that. I intend to speak to the Führer personally about it, and I'll make it my business to arrange for Operation Cicero to be handled entirely by this department."

So the great men in Berlin were squabbling about Cicero. They were tearing each other's hair out, quarrelling about whether or not my documents had been planted on them by the British and whether or not I was a reliable spy. But in Ankara I was not so much Cicero the spy as Elyesa the snooping *kavass*, and how was I to know how much I was exercising these people's minds?

How was I to know that at that time there was in Berne, in Switzerland, an American named Allen W. Dulles, who for a long time had had plenty of informants in Berlin? How was I to know that one of those informants was a German diplomatist in Ribbentrop's entourage, whose brother the Nazis had beaten to death? Only after the war did I find out that he informed Mr. Dulles in Berne of the existence of a new spy named Cicero who must be active in the British Embassy in Ankara.

The Americans jumped at Cicero. Would it not be an intense pleasure to serve up the solved problem of Cicero on a plate to their British allies with the clear implication that the latter had been fast asleep? Thus Cicero became a plaything of the rival security services, whose self-esteem was at stake.

The Americans called in their Balkan specialist, George H. Earle. I could be proud of being the cause of headaches to Mr. Earle, who was a personal friend of President Roosevelt's. I, a *kavass*, was beginning to have world-wide repercussions.

Mr. Earle, former governor of Pennsylvania, former American envoy in Vienna and Sofia, and finally Military Attaché in Istanbul, thought of a woman member of the American secret service in Sofia. Might it not be possible to smuggle her into the German Embassy in Ankara?

This young woman was Cornelia Kapp. The cover-name Cicero had travelled by way of Berlin, Berne, Washington, Istanbul and Sofia back to Ankara, had been the subject of excited gossip and heated altercation, of admiration, doubt and mistrust, only to end up in a secret, underground struggle in neutral Ankara, where the diplomatists of hostile countries greeted each other with icy reserve.

I, of course, knew nothing of all this, and least of all did I know that a young woman of twenty-three was on my trail and risking her neck in the process.

I used to hate Cornelia Kapp, but my hatred is now nearly twenty years old, and it is no longer very fresh or vivid. Sometimes I wonder what would happen if we met.

"Good heavens, are you Cicero?"

I can see very plainly the disappointment on her face.

"None of us is getting any younger, madam."

112

I have often imagined a conversation of this kind between two people who were once engaged in a great adventure on opposite sides.

Is it possible to revive a hatred that has grown old and stale? Would I really say to her: "Madame, you were disloyal to your country, I regard you with contempt"? And would she really answer: "Rubbish, Cicero, I acted out of conviction, and you spied for money, and it is only in retrospect that you behave as if you understood world politics and wanted to correct the course of history"?

Would our conversation really take that course?

No doubt in practice I should inquire after her two children, and she would politely and ironically ask after mine.

"I have heard that you have six children, Cicero. Is that true?"

"No, madam, I have eight. I admit madam, that it seems ridiculous for a former spy to have eight children. But I assure you that it is a fact that I have taken my youngest daughter on my knee and said to her: 'And then your daddy got hold of the key of Sir Hughe Knatchbull-Hugessen's safe, and . . .' "

However, if I had known her to be my enemy at the time, I should not have hesitated to say to Moyzisch: "You have an enemy in your ranks. Her name is Cornelia Kapp, and she is your secretary."

And that would have been equivalent to a death sentence on Cornelia Kapp.

But all I knew about her then was her voice on the telephone. Not until years later did I find out anything more.

She was said to be living in America. I wrote to friends there, but with no result. They said that in a huge country like the United States there was no hope of tracking down a woman who was no doubt married and had been living for years under her husband's name. I wrote to the immigration authorities, but they did not even trouble to reply.

However, when we were preparing this book we asked the journalist G. Thomas Beyl to assist in our researches, and he it was who tracked down Cornelia, starting by discovering that she had once stayed in Chicago with Mr. and Mrs. Hugo Coutandin.

A correspondence with the Coutandins followed, which helped me to build up the picture of Cornelia that I wanted. I was given another address, of a restaurant in Chicago, where, I was told, Cornelia had worked as a waitress. I was told that her best friend there was a girl named Violet Kyle, known as Pinky.

Pinky reported: "I still work in the restaurant, but Cornelia left a long time ago. The proprietor took Cornelia because she was German. He was a German who deserted during the First World War and lived here with false papers. But that came to light only when he committed suicide a short time ago. . . . In any case he helped Cornelia to find her feet here. Cornelia is—or was—married to a former F.B.I. agent. She met him at the Coutandins. They both lodged there. I can give you the name of the town in California where they live."

Beyl went to California, saw Cornelia, and got her statement.

I read through all the information I had gathered. I read

what the Coutandins had to say, I read Pinky's letter, and I read what Cornelia herself had to say about the "Cicero business." And that was how I discovered that she had not been, as I had always supposed, a British agent, but an American one, as I have narrated above.

CHAPTER 6

The arrival of the British security men from London had consequences. An alarm system was built into Sir Hughe's safe. Specialists arrived, disappeared into the offices, and worked there for hours behind locked doors; and I could only imagine what they were doing. I decided that the duplicate key to Sir Hughe's safe would no longer be of any use.

I took this as a hint from destiny. I was ready to cause the spy Cicero to vanish. I removed the money that I had kept for weeks hidden under the carpet of my room, and then, after Mara's warning, under the basement steps. I took it to my rented house, and I locked it in the desk. I decided that now I was rich enough to retire. I was under no obligation to go on with my dangerous game.

I need only destroy the photographic apparatus and cover my tracks. But I could not bring myself to do it. I kept putting it off. I waited, without being able to say what for.

I met Moyzisch, but without having anything to hand over to him. I explained that things were too difficult at the moment.

I could not shake off my lethargy. I had the strength neither to stop nor to go on.

"The air raid on Sofia took place," Moyzisch said in a toneless voice.

I shrugged my shoulders. "I told you it would," I said.

I did not know that there were people in Berlin who still doubted the genuineness of my documents.

Of the raid on Sofia Moyzisch later wrote: "I wondered if Berlin was satisfied now. They had their proof. Cicero was genuine. Four thousand Bulgarians, men, women and children, had vouched for it with their lives."

To me Moyzisch said: "Now everyone will believe your material is genuine."

I did not care whether they believed it or not.

"Don't you want to go on?" Moyzisch asked.

"I don't know."

The freezing cold of the misty winter day did not improve matters.

I went to my house, but Mara was hysterical. She overwhelmed me with her tirades, which were the outcome of fear and jealousy.

"Mrs. Busk is moving to London soon for the sake of the baby. She has asked me to go with her," she said.

"Then for heaven's sake go."

Mara looked at me with staring eyes.

"I knew it!" she exclaimed. "I knew it! Everything has been over between us for a long time! You're sending me away!"

I could not bear listening to her.

"It was you who first mentioned going away," I said. "It was you who first talked of going to London."

"You don't want to have anything more to do with me!"

This sort of thing drove me out of the house. I went to the Embassy. The rooms were delightfully warm. Quiet, comfort, civilisation, the atmosphere of an English country house. Strange to relate, I felt a sense of peace in the Embassy, as if it were my only haven of rest.

Sir Hughe's unchanged friendliness towards me made me feel ashamed, and my servant's room was like a little oasis. I envied Mustafa his life as a carefree *kavass*. Had I not once been like him?

I lay down on my bed and lulled myself with the dream of a modest, quiet, danger-free life.

Mustafa came into the room, grinning from ear to ear and rolling his eyes. There was an expression of rapture on his face.

"Oh, Allah!" he exclaimed. "She has arrived! Esra is here!"

I had totally forgotten having written to Cousin Mehmet, telling him to send Esra to Ankara, because I had a job in mind for her.

Esra's arrival put an end to all my sensible intentions.

I was twenty years older than Esra. That is the only excuse that I can think of.

I was conceited, shameless, sentimental, cynical, superstitious, ugly, and full of complexes. I was burning with ambition, and felt very sorry for myself. I possessed no qualities strong enough to cause me to send Esra back to her father.

She was seventeen, and fair, like many Turks of Greek origin. She was a pliable creature, and she had a provoking laugh, as if she were aware of her attractiveness. She melted the hearts of Manoli Filoti, Mustafa, and even the butler

Zeki. She brought life into the servants' quarters, kept the male staff on its toes, and allowed herself to be tickled, flattered and spoilt. She had escaped from the supervision of her parents, and she enjoyed her freedom. It infuriated me to think of Mustafa's being near her when I was busy with Sir Hughe, and so I treated her unkindly and sarcastically.

"I don't know whether there will be a job here for you," I told her. "You dress badly, and you're too loud."

"Mustafa said . . ."

"Mustafa is not successful with women, he's only too glad when he finds one that likes him."

"But I don't like him."

"I can't help that. You can go out with him if you like. I've got no time for you, I'm too busy."

"But I want you to tell me what I do wrong."

"I told you I was too busy."

Treating her like this was my only weapon against her youth. She was given Manoli's room.

I frowned. "I don't think Lady Knatchbull-Hugessen will allow you to go on staying here. I think I'd better write to your father. . . ."

"I don't want to go home! Please, please, don't have me sent home!"

"Then you must go to the hairdresser's and have your hair done properly."

Her hair was wonderful. I loved its fair shimmer. My derogatory remarks made her unsure of herself.

I saw her helpless expression when she looked at me. I could tell that all the flattery and compliments lavished on her by others had no effect on her whatever, and that all she cared about was getting a good word from me. The girl had taken possession of me, and I forced myself to ignore her.

I was pressing Sir Hughe's suits in the ironing room when the current suddenly failed.

I went to the fuse-box. Esra was there already.

"A fuse must have blown," I said. "Go and ask Mustafa for a new one."

"No," she said, "none of the fuses have blown. I've had to take them out."

I stared at her, and she gave me the explanation.

"Some workmen are here," she said. "They're working on the safe where the money's kept. I was told to take out the fuses. . . ."

I did not wait for the rest of the story. What Esra took to be the safe where the money was kept was the safe where secret documents were kept. I hurried to the room.

An Embassy official who belonged to the security service was sitting with a bored expression on his face, watching two workmen who were busy with the safe.

"Is it necessary to have the fuses removed?" I said coolly. "I need some current, or Sir Hughe will be angry."

The safe door was open. The men were working on the alarm system, and they took no notice of me.

"Very well then, I'll put all the fuses back immediately!" I said angrily, and turned to leave.

This worked like a charm. One of the workmen came sulkily after me.

"What are you getting so upset about?"

"I've got to do my ironing."

"Where are the fuses?"

I took him to them. Esra was still standing there.

"If you've got to repair the alarm system," I said coldly, "it's sufficient to remove the fuse connected with it."

"That's my business," the man grumbled.

He had to go backwards and forwards several times before he found out which was the right fuse. Then he put the others back.

"After all, you don't have to cut off the current all over the house just because your alarm bell won't work!" I said with a grin.

The workman went back to the room. I looked at Esra.

"Note that fuse," I said.

She was puzzled.

"Why?"

"I just want you to note it, that's all."

My shameless self-confidence had been restored. I felt that the streak of luck which I thought had deserted me had returned.

I could do anything when I felt I was being admired, and Esra was beginning to admire me.

"I have a problem for you," I said to her. "What is the use of fitting up a safe with an alarm system if all that is necessary to put the alarm bell out of action is to remove an easily accessible fuse?"

"I don't understand," she murmured.

"I'll explain this evening."

I left her standing in front of the fuse boxes and went back to the ironing room. The iron was hot again.

We were sitting muffled up in a taxi.

"Drive through the Old Town, past the Citadel, then to the Atatürk Boulevard, and then to the hills."

I enjoyed nonchalantly giving orders to the taxi-man and feeling Esra by my side.

I showed her the sights of Ankara by night. My voice was cool, as if I were carrying out a troublesome duty. I knew that her thoughts were elsewhere.

"Why did you buy me that coat?"

She asked the question quietly and soberly. We had gone to the A.B.C., and I had bought her a beautiful, soft, fur-lined coat.

"I don't like your old one," I answered casually. "You must take some trouble if you want to look pretty. That's the Citadel, over there."

She looked, but was not interested. She still had the coat on her mind.

"It was terribly expensive," she said.

"Don't trouble your head about that."

I was a complete puzzle to her. I treated her casually, almost rudely, but then gave her an expensive present.

We drove down the brightly lit Atatürk Boulevard. The cab glided silently over the snow.

I had to exercise a great deal of self-control to prevent myself from putting my arms around Esra, but that would have spoilt everything. The streets grew quieter. We drove through the smart villa quarter and out of the city.

The Siberian winter that prevails in Anatolia was at its height. The hills were covered with snow. The night sky overhead was cold and clear.

I told the driver to stop and wait for us. "We'll walk for a bit," I said to Esra.

I walked beside her, my hands stuck deep in my overcoat

pockets. I did not look at the girl. In the distance there was a muffled, threatening howl.

"Wolves," I said. "In winter they come to the very edge of the city. Are you freezing?"

I had noticed her shivering.

"No," she muttered.

"What do you think of this war?"

She looked at me in a puzzled way.

"What has it to do with us?"

"You're quite right," I said. "You too think that we must keep out of it."

"I don't understand anything about . . ."

"Would you like to go to the university?"

My question took her by surprise. To a modern Turkish girl nothing seems more desirable than going to the university. In Turkey women still count for nothing as a rule, but a girl who goes to the university feels herself to be free, modern, and European.

Esra dropped her head. She was gradually falling for my gifts.

"I have always wanted to study," she whispered.

The snow crunched under our feet.

"Do you still remember which fuse to remove?"

She looked at me silently.

I said: "If you still remember, one day you'll be able to go to the university. Or do you just want to remain a female *kavass?*"

"I don't understand about the fuse."

I took time to answer. I let the quiet and our lonely footsteps do the work for me.

"Can't you imagine?"

I said this coolly and casually. Then I stopped still in front of the girl.

"Money is not kept in that safe," I said. "War secrets are kept in it."

To Esra I was a dark, squat shadow against the white, shimmering hillside. I was play-acting, and was completely at home in my role.

If I had kissed her, she would not have thought me ugly and revolting, but the very embodiment of thrilling adventure. But I looked at her quietly and did not move.

I said: "You must realise that it involves everything. Come along!"

We walked slowly back to the cab. To Esra it was a night of cold romance and fascinating danger.

"Do you hand over everything to the Germans?" she asked in childish, eager tones.

"That has nothing to do with you."

We got into the cab. Esra sat stiff and upright in the corner.

I smoked. I felt perfectly sure of myself. I heard the girl swallowing.

Then she spoke very softly.

"I'm not sure which fuse it is," she said.

"I'll have to make up my mind whether I can use you or not," I replied.

This was the evening of the fourth day after Esra's arrival.

The word "Overlord" kept cropping up in the documents I photographed. There was practically no doubt that this was a cover-name for the second front for which the Russians

were pressing their allies—that is to say, the invasion of
Normandy.

It became possible to discern the intentions of Roosevelt,
Stalin and Churchill.

Churchill wanted Turkey to intervene in the war. He
planned an invasion of Greece; he wanted to take Salonika
with Turkish support and invade the Balkans, so that the
western allies as well as the Russians should have a foot-
hold there.

But the Turks were hesitant about becoming active partners of the British. They said that they would not intervene
until after the successful invasion of France. The British
wanted Turkish intervention and the invasion of Greece to
precede the invasion of France. That was the crude reading
of the situation that I derived from the documents. The
question was whether British pressure or Turkish delaying
tactics would win the diplomatic battle.

Esra quickly saw the light. On the day after our expedi-
tion to the snow-covered hills she came to my room.

"Sir Hughe has gone out to lunch," she said.

I could not help smiling, because of course I knew that.

"How do you know?" I said.

"I saw him driving away. Manoli told me he would be
out for lunch."

She paused. I had won her over so completely that she
wanted to give me a surprise.

"His secretary is out too," she said.

I rose to my feet.

"Perhaps she has only gone out for a short walk," I said.

Esra shook her head.

"You made me go to the hairdresser's. . . ."

I noticed her new hair-do for the first time. I looked at her attentively.

". . . and when I came out she walked in. It takes a long time at the hairdresser's."

Had I been only boasting to myself during the past few days? Was fear getting hold of me again, now that I was faced with the decision whether or not to open the safe that was now provided with an alarm system?

I smiled. I did not let Esra see what I was feeling.

"Very well, then," I said slowly. "Remove the fuse."

I could see how excited she was. I could see the tension in her face. But she managed to return my smile.

"There's no need to remove it," she said. "I've done it already."

CHAPTER 7

I had a moment of self-revelation. I realised what my real motive had been in bringing Esra to the Embassy. I wanted to have her there, not as an assistant, but as an audience.

Mara in her time had served the same purpose. The stimulus that drove me on had been the fear and trembling and admiration I roused in her. But performing acts of recklessness for her benefit had lost its savour, and that was why Esra was now so welcome. I was like an actor in a new town, before a new, critical audience which had to be won over, whose applause had first to be earned. My need to make an impression was too strong for my fear; my fear simply could not compete with it.

I felt like a hero in a spy play; Esra was an admiring spectator in the box who would afterwards ask for my autograph.

"Wait outside my room."

I looked at her coolly and collectedly.

"Yes," she whispered.

Her waiting there served no useful purpose, but it was part of the spy game I was playing. How could Esra help me by waiting in the corridor? What good would it do if she shouted: "Look out, somebody's coming!" What I wanted her there for was to show her how cool and collected I could be while performing a reckless feat of daring. Her shining eyes spurred me on. Acting cold-blooded confidence made me cold-blooded and confident.

As I walked up the stairs to the room where the safe was I felt her eyes on me.

What could happen to me? Sir Hughe was at an official luncheon. Louise, his secretary, was at the hairdresser's. Lady Knatchbull-Hugessen had been invisible all the morning. She was keeping to her quarters, nursing a cold with fantastic quantities of tea.

I walked into the room without looking round. Without hesitation I opened the safe. I took the documents from the red box, closed the safe, and went back to my room, whistling *Je suis seul ce soir*.

Esra stared at me blankly as I passed her. I took no notice of her.

I took my photographs.

The documents were a Foreign Office directive concerning the information to be given to the Turkish Government in connection with the allied war plans for 1944. I discovered that an operation was projected against the German positions in the Balkans, that is to say, an invasion of Greece:

"It is proposed that British bomber and fighter squadrons be allowed to land on February 15 at the Izmir air base to provide effective support for the operation against Salonika from that base. It is to be impressed on the Turkish Government that they must consent to this operation and help to carry it out."

This meant Turkish intervention, Turkish involvement in the war. But more important to me at that moment were the words of admiration that a girl of seventeen would address to me when I shared my omniscience with her.

I had to hold the camera in my hand to take these photographs. I had left my "tripod" with the money in "Villa Cicero," the little house among the hills of Kavaklidere of which I was so proud.

I hid the documents under my livery.

In the corridor I said to Esra: "Put the fuse back in five minutes. I shan't be longer than that."

I walked slowly up the stairs, taking my time in order not to diminish Esra's admiration by any show of nervous haste, and I paid for my recklessness with a terrible fright.

"Elyesa!" a voice called out. It was Lady Knatchbull-Hugessen.

I had not seen her. Her voice shattered my trance-like self-confidence, and I stood rooted to the spot. I stared blankly at this woman, whose alertness intimidated me more than any frown of her Ambassador husband's. Was it her cold that blinded her to my trembling?

"What about that girl relative of yours? Have you found her a job yet?"

I had forgotten that Esra was only a temporary guest of Lady Knatchbull-Hugessen's.

"Not yet, madam," I stammered out. "I thought that perhaps she might be able to work here, because . . ."

"I told you that she could stay here only temporarily. I must ask you to find somewhere else for her to stay."

She was used to giving orders.

"Of course, madam. I'll see to it immediately."

129

The fright, which first froze me, now brought the sweat to my brow. Lady Knatchbull-Hugessen was rapidly using up what was left of my five minutes.

"I don't like my good nature to be imposed upon."

How much time had passed? I tried desperately to work it out.

"Madam, I would not presume . . . Esra will leave the Embassy today. You can rest assured, madam . . ."

Had Esra put the fuse back yet? Would the alarm bell go off when I put the documents back in the safe?

"Ask Mustafa to bring up another pot of tea."

"I'll tell him immediately, madam."

I turned as if to go to the kitchen. Her voice called me back.

"Esra needn't go today," she said in a more friendly manner. "But she can't stay here indefinitely."

She nodded at me, and stalked off towards her room.

I gazed after her.

"I am much obliged to you, madam," I murmured, and walked into the room where the safe was. It did not occur to me that it would have been more prudent to find out first whether or not Esra had put back the fuse. All I wanted was to get rid of the documents.

I opened the safe, put the papers back in the box, and closed the safe again. The alarm system remained silent.

I went down to the kitchen.

"Tea for her ladyship!" I muttered.

Mustafa stared at me. "Are you feeling all right?" he exclaimed.

"You're to take up her tea!" I yelled at him. I could no longer control myself. I went out, slamming the door behind me.

130

There was a helpless, guilty expression on Esra's face. At first I did not notice it.

"The fuse broke when I tried to put it back," she whispered.

So I had someone on whom to vent my rage. The fact that I probably owed everything to the breaking of that fuse made no difference.

"Then get a new one!" I shouted at her.

"It wasn't my fault," she stammered, as if she had been caught red-handed committing a crime.

"I've got no more use for you!" I yelled at her. "You can't stay in the Embassy a moment longer!"

I felt that my legs were giving way beneath me.

Esra dropped her head, and so did not notice the panic I was in.

Next time I met Moyzisch, not in his car, but in his office, at his request. We took the same precautions as on my first visit. Once more I crept through the hole in the fence behind the tool-shed in the German Embassy grounds.

I was received by Herr Jenke, Ribbentrop's brother-in-law.

"Moyzisch will be here in a moment," he said.

He smiled. I seemed to read in his eyes a certain amount of appreciation of my services.

"If the Germans don't prevent it, Turkey will soon be in the war," I said to him, and told him what was in the films I had brought.

"Then we shall have to make strong representations to the Turkish Government immediately," he muttered.

It was on this occasion that he mentioned that Hitler proposed to present me with a villa in Germany after the end of the war. This was a prospect highly pleasing to my self-esteem, because physical comfort is always welcome to a *kavass*.

At this point Moyzisch appeared, and I handed over the film.

Papen later wrote in his memoirs:

"Cicero's information was immensely valuable for two reasons. A résumé of the decisions taken at the Teheran conference was sent to the British Ambassador. This revealed the Allies' intentions concerning the political treatment of Germany after her defeat, and showed us where the differences between the Allies lay. But what was of greater and even more immediate importance was the intimate knowledge he gave us of the enemy's operational plans."

They obtained their intimate knowledge through me, but would they be able to keep Turkey out of the war?

I felt myself to be champion of the Turkish cause, though an uninvited champion.

"I am acting on my country's behalf," I said grandiloquently to Esra, carried away by my sense of my own importance; and I added vaingloriously: "True, I am paid enormous sums for my services—but by a foreign state. It is not the Turkish Treasury that I am impoverishing."

Esra listened to me in awe. After I had convinced her that she was not intelligent or quick-witted enough to be my assistant, she read my slightest wishes in my eyes. I was a great man in the eyes of an adoring little girl.

I bought her clothes as a thanks-offering for the fact that the alarm-bell had not gone off, and she accepted the present as the magnanimous gesture of a hero who, in her opinion, had every reason to spurn and be angry with her.

As it was impossible for her to remain in the Embassy, I told her I would put her up in "Villa Cicero."

"Oh, I'm so glad!" she exclaimed.

"Why?" I asked coolly.

"I was afraid you were going to send me back to my parents."

"I ought to," I said grimly. "There's probably going to be war."

"I want to stay with you," she murmured with downcast eyes.

I pretended not to hear.

"We shall know by February 15," I said.

"Can't it be prevented?" she asked childishly.

"Perhaps I may have prevented it already," I said conceitedly. "But I don't know for certain yet."

I greatly enjoyed the awe with which she looked up at me.

It was a grotesque situation. I was familiar with the plans of great men in whose hands lay the destinies of nations. I pried into secrets on which life and death depended—and at the same time watched with a mocking leer the ridiculous duel between my new girl Esra and Mara, her predecessor, who was reluctant to surrender her place.

"If you bring that girl into the house I'll go to London with Mrs. Busk," she announced.

As if I cared! I no longer had the slightest fear of Mara. She was too weak to avenge herself by giving me away. She had been on the retreat for a long time, and all that she was really doing now was fighting a delaying action. Secretly she was probably quite satisfied with the situation. Had I not given her plenty of money?

I took Esra to the house. We went by taxi, with a trunk on board as well as a cardboard box from the A.B.C. with the new clothes I had bought her.

"You dare!" Mara exclaimed.

I could not help laughing, and that finally shook off the effects of the fright that Lady Knatchbull-Hugessen had given me.

"You behave as if she were my girl-friend," I said to Mara.

The grotesque situation lasted for ten days. Those ten days were fantastic. I was Sir Hughe's attentive valet, and I daily photographed his secret documents. His wife was friendly towards me, because I had so promptly carried out her wishes. Turkish intervention in the war hung in the balance. At night I was a spy taking his ease in his slippers, a pasha condescendingly accepting the attentions of rival odalisques, who flattered his vanity, broke all records in the preparation of his favourite dishes, and massaged his body and soul, valiantly competing for their master's favour in the celebrations that followed yet another successful espionage *coup*.

"Was she your mistress?" Esra asked.

"That's no business of yours."

Mara said: "Mrs. Busk has again asked me to go with her to London. What do you want me to do?"

"London must be a wonderful city," I replied.

It was the question of Turkish intervention that was settled first. Papen intervened successfully with the Turkish Government. His knowledge of secret agreements, which he had obtained through me and which so much astonished the Ankara Government, enabled the Turks to extricate themselves from the bloody business. The answer that the Turkish Foreign Minister, Numan Menemencioglu, handed to the British Ambassador was no. I photographed it.

Papen wrote later:

"Thanks to Cicero, the Turkish Government's reply to the Allies dated December 12 lay on my desk a few days later. Mr. Menemencioglu declared that in view of the totally insufficient flow of supplies to the Turkish forces it would be quite impossible to complete the preparations for the Salonika operation by the middle of February. This note proved a grave disappointment to the Western Allies. . . ."

He also wrote:

"Hitler was thus fully informed by me of the fact that the Churchillian offensive against Salonika in February would not take place. . . . On February 3 the British military mission left Turkey. Significantly enough, Air Marshal Linnell, who was to be in charge of the preparations for the attack on Salonika arranged for February 15, also left the country, disappointed. . . . The Balkan operation had to be abandoned."

At the British Embassy I was able to observe how angry the British Ambassador was at all this, however much he tried to conceal his feelings from me, a mere member of the domestic staff.

I had photographed the telegram containing the text of the Turkish refusal which Sir Hughe sent to London. His anger was also perceptible in the dispatches to London that I photographed in which he proposed breaking off relations with Ankara. I knew what was going on in his mind when I handed him his orange juice or one of his carefully brushed suits, though outwardly he remained the cool and reserved gentleman.

I photographed all the documents, and I felt immense relief at the removal of the threat of war from my country. The part I had played in it made me feel proud and self-important.

Before Sir Hughe went to say good-bye to Air Marshal Linnell I handed him the suit he wanted to wear.

"It's a wonderful day today, Your Excellency," I said.

"If you only knew how uninterested I am in the weather," he replied. He looked extremely depressed. How was he to know that I was not referring to the weather?

He too later wrote his memoirs. Of this period he said: "A period of some difficulty followed, during which we made no attempt to conceal our disappointment."

While Sir Hughe was saying good-bye to Air Marshal Linnell I was wiping the tears from Mara's cheeks. She remained loyal to Mrs. Busk and her baby, and accompanied them to England.

"I'm not angry with you," she said, with the feminine bravery which enables a man to make a display of emotion in a dignified manner.

That night Esra became my mistress.

One day many years later, long after our romance and passion were spent, I met Esra again. We talked, and she said with a smile: "You gave Mara her marching orders, and you could twist me round your little finger. But you didn't bother your head about the woman who really mattered to you. You didn't even know that Cornelia existed."

I told her how I had since made up for the omission.

From the Coutandins and the waitress Pinky in Chicago, and from Cornelia herself in California, I had learned why she played the part she did, and what had happened to her. But I still felt that she was a shadowy figure—sometimes I could hardly believe that she had existed. What had she been thinking, feeling, doing during that time when we were the most important part of each other's lives but did not know each other? Although the information I wanted was no longer of any practical value, I began to pry into Cornelia's life as I had once pried into Ribbentrop's brother-in-law's letters, and later into Sir Hughe's safe and the black box by his bed.

The obvious people to approach were those who worked with her at the German Embassy in Ankara: Moyzisch and his colleagues. I could not afford the fare to Germany, to visit them, and anyway my German was not good enough to make an interview worth while. Herr Nogly put me in touch with a newspaperman, Hans Schwarz, and he it was who discovered for me how Cornelia had struck the colleagues whom she had been betraying.

Our chief source of information was a man called Seiler, who had been Herr von Papen's press attaché and who knew Moyzisch very well. Moyzisch and I had once met in his flat; it was there that I handed over the film that showed that the British plans to invade Greece and capture Salonika had been abandoned. Seiler was a tall, broad-shouldered, auburn-haired man, and the occasion was not one of the exciting, cloak-and-dagger meetings such as we had in Moyzisch's car: it was more like a social occasion. We drank whisky and things got very gay. Moyzisch said, à propos of a piano in the room, "You said you sang to Sir Hughe's accompaniment. Can you really sing?"

"You Germans are never satisfied," I said. "You require proof of everything." I sang a few arias, to the accompaniment of clinking glasses as well as of the piano.

It was Seiler who had actually brought Cornelia to Ankara. He now lives near Nuremberg, and he no longer has a piano; he has become a chicken farmer. One of the pieces of the mosaic I put together to build up a picture of Cornelia consisted of the tape-recording of Herr Schwarz's interview with him.

I sat in my flat in Istanbul, an ex-spy trying to conjure up the past. On the walls were photographs of me, Bazna, in a number of the roles that I have played. In particular there was a photograph of me as a concert singer, in evening dress. Testimonials to my conceit. I lounged in my flowery easy chair, bored with the respectable life I was leading, and listened to information that had a very great bearing on my past life, elicited by questions that were answerable now but were not at the time. I also listened to the thoughts provoked in me by listening to the tape-recording. The solid comfort of my little room seemed to disappear. During the pauses the noise made by the tape got on my nerves. It was as if everything was taking place at the time when it was still a matter of vital and acute concern to me.

"What were your duties in the German Embassy in Ankara in 1944?"

"I was the press attaché."

"What were your relations with Moyzisch?"

"We were friends."

"Did you work with him?"

"When the occasion arose."

"How was it that Cornelia became Moyzisch's secretary?"

"It was by pure chance."

"A very remarkable chance. Wasn't it you who brought her to Ankara?"

"Moyzisch urgently needed more staff. He had one secretary, and was looking for another."

"Because Cicero's reports were giving him a great deal of work?"

"Yes."

"So he sent you to Sofia and told you to look round for a suitable secretary, and you happened to hit on Cornelia. I suppose you know that she had already worked for the Americans in Sofia?"

"How was I to know that? You've got it all wrong. Moyzisch did not send me to Sofia to find a secretary. The whole thing happened by pure chance when I went to Sofia for my press office."

"What for?"

"To buy things—teleprinter supplies, copying material, and so on, all of which were very difficult to get at the time in Berlin and were very cheap in Sofia. . . ."

"Did Cornelia approach you?"

"I stayed at the Bulgari Hotel, which was reserved for Germans. Members of the Embassy staff lived there, members of trade delegations, and officers on missions of various kinds."

"And that was where Cornelia Kapp was staying?"

"Yes."

"Again by pure chance?"

"She was there with her parents. Her father was a consul-general attached to the German Embassy."

"And?"

"She was working as a secretary in the Embassy."

"Thanks to her father."

"She was very efficient. Everybody confirmed it."

"Elyesa Bazna, *alias* Cicero, found out to his cost how efficient she was."

"I met her parents in the hotel lounge. Nice, decent, honest people. Kapp was a diplomatist of the old school. He had been consul-general at Bombay and later at Cleveland, Ohio, and . . ."

"Yes, I know. How old was he?"

"In his fifties. A conscientious man, very kind-hearted. . . ."

"Particularly to his daughter."

"That's true enough. I had the impression that he was willing to fulfil her slightest whim."

"Including the whim to act as a traitor to her country in Ankara?"

"What could he do about that? I make no judgment on the girl."

"She was attractive, wasn't she?"

"Yes, very. She was just over twenty, I think."

"It's difficult to form an adverse opinion of a pretty girl of that age."

The tape-recording went on and on, and there I sat in Istanbul, listening to the reminiscences of the chicken-breeder Seiler. I could well imagine how the kindly and conscientious Herr Kapp idolised his favourite daughter, the attractive blonde who was out to destroy me.

"Was Cornelia always present when you talked to Herr Kapp?"

"Yes, that is correct."

"No doubt she arranged to be present."

"There was no sign of that. Kapp asked me whether there might not be a job for her in Ankara. Turkey was a neutral country, after all, and heavy air raids on Sofia were expected."

"Which you knew, thanks to Cicero."

"There was a general impression abroad among German diplomatists in Sofia that things were going to get unpleasant there."

"Oh, I see! Cicero's reports were evidently kept very secret."

There was a long pause, and all that was to be heard was the running of the tape. In my mind's eye I could see Seiler shrugging his shoulders. Had he talked too much at the time? Moyzisch must have told him all sorts of things. Had not the two of them driven me straight into Cornelia's arms? I seethed with belated anger. The recording interrupted my train of thought.

"So you told Kapp that your friend Moyzisch, the agent of the *Sicherheitsamt* who was handling the famous Operation Cicero, was so busy at the moment that he could well do with Cornelia's help."

"No, it didn't happen like that."

"How did it happen, then?"

"I told him there might be a job for his daughter in Ankara, and said I would see what I could do about it. I knew how desperately Moyzisch needed more help."

"So you walked straight into the trap?"

"You are assuming that Herr Kapp was in league with Cornelia."

"Why should he not have been?"

"He was a man of honour. Later he was desperately unhappy when he found out about Cornelia, and he died of grief."

"So first she led her father up the garden path, and then you."

"My only concern was to oblige a senior colleague in whom I had complete confidence. I told Herr Kapp that the post I had in mind required complete discretion and reliability."

"And no doubt Cornelia called out: 'Then that's just the job for me!'"

"She didn't say anything at all. She just sat there without opening her mouth. It was Herr Kapp who answered. He said that no doubt the daughter of a Foreign Service official of long standing would be a suitable person."

"And you told him that she would be involved in Operation Cicero?"

"I told him nothing of the sort."

"You mean to say that you didn't mention Operation Cicero, which was talked about in German diplomatic circles as much as Goebbels's love affairs?"

"I never mentioned Cicero. Only . . ."

"Only what?"

"Well, I mentioned in conversation that we had certain sources of information. But I never mentioned that in Kapp's presence. Only to other people in Sofia."

"Did you ever go out with Cornelia?"

"Good heavens, don't make it so romantic! I went back to Ankara and told Moyzisch I had found just the right girl for him. The daughter of a consul-general who had been brought up in America and spoke English like her mother-tongue. Moyzisch said: 'I must get hold of her, I must get hold of her.' "

"Why was he so eager?"

"He's very impulsive in his attractive Austrian way."

"And so she came to Ankara."

"First she was screened. By the personnel department of the Foreign Ministry, and by the *Sicherheitsamt*. In the last resort the job was part of the Kaltenbrunner set-up."

"And they all thought that Cornelia was the right person for it?"

"She arrived in Ankara in January, 1944."

How triumphant my enemy must have felt when she brought it off! However, the tape-recording produced a surprise.

"I went to the station with Moyzisch to meet her. When she got out of the compartment I had a shock."

"Why?"

"I had recommended her, and I had described her as very pretty, very attractive, and very well dressed. When she got out of the train she was such a sight that Moyzisch looked at me as if he doubted I were in my right mind."

"She made a bad impression?"

"She looked appalling. She was a bundle of nerves. Her hair was hanging down over her face, and her hands and finger-nails were filthy."

"But after a long railway journey. . . ."

"Oh no, it wasn't that, it wasn't that at all. I had the

143

impression that something must have happened during the journey that had affected her so much that she had completely lost interest in her personal appearance."

"Perhaps she had some sort of crisis and wanted to get out of the spy business. Perhaps the Americans for whom she was working got at her during the journey. Perhaps she was under pressure. She had let herself in for something, and perhaps she had changed her mind and wanted to get out of it, and pressure was put on her. . . ."

"I don't know. At the time we were completely baffled by her appearance and behaviour."

"Did she change later?"

"Outwardly she certainly did. Moyzisch remonstrated with her about the way she was going about, and she swallowed it. But I think she hated him for offending her feminine pride. But, quite apart from that . . ."

"What?"

"She was difficult to handle. She was completely apathetic and never smiled or laughed. Just the opposite of what she was like in Sofia. She was a totally different person. Moyzisch said that perhaps we ought to find her a man, perhaps that was the trouble. Her hysteria made things very difficult. . . ."

The tape-recording came to an end. The questions that I had caused to be asked had produced answers which showed me a Cornelia I had not expected—a beautiful girl, a desperate girl, a highly astute girl and a hysterical girl, who neglected her personal appearance and later paid exaggerated attention to it.

The letter accompanying the recording said that another tape was to follow.

The girl was evidently a riddle, not only to me, but to the people in closest contact with her.

I turned back to the correspondence from California, and to Cornelia Kapp's own statements. She said:

"My hysterical behaviour was no more than a diversionary manoeuvre on my part. I acted hysteria to disguise my real nervousness and restlessness. After all, I was living in perpetual fear of being caught, and if I had behaved normally I should only have attracted attention to myself on the days when the tension became almost intolerable. But, as it was, I appeared to be hysterical all the time."

So the Cornelia who was trying to catch me acted the hysteric just as I acted the cold-blooded spy in front of Esra. In retrospect I felt the kinship of our two characters.

There was one passage in her statement that alarmed me. She said:

"While I was in Ankara I had to take strong drugs, because my work was a terrible nervous strain. I knew that my father's excellent connections in Berlin would not have saved me from the gallows if I had been caught."

Had she really been only play-acting for the benefit of others? Was it not really herself she was deceiving when she lulled her conscience and her fear with drugs?

I sat in my bourgeois comfort, surrounded by correspondence, tape-recordings, and Turkish knick-knacks. How would it be if the door suddenly opened and Cornelia walked in, now in her late thirties and, like me, past her prime?

I should say: "Let us both admit that it was a dirty business. They used us just as I used my camera. Did it really give us any satisfaction? Did we really feel so important?

145

Most of the time we spent hiding the fact that we were afraid."

Would Cornelia admit it?

I would smile with my mouth awry, and say: "What did they tell you to try and make you forget our fear?"

CHAPTER **8**

The hopes and fears of a world at war were concentrated in the mysterious phrase Operation Overlord. To General Staffs it was a mathematical problem, to secret services it was a riddle, to the enemy it was a mortal threat. To every one of the 176,000 officers and men involved it might mean death.

It was to begin on a day known as D-day, the exact date of which was not finally fixed. But there were only a few possible dates for the event on which the Allies had set all their hopes. Success depended on the coincidence of a number of factors.

In the first place the preceding night must be moonlit. Then the tide must be right, and the sea must not be too rough. The 176,000 men who that day would cross the English Channel with their 20,000 vehicles, men just as afraid of death as all men are, must be prepared to forget their fear. They must establish themselves on the coasts of Normandy or die.

The nervous strain of waiting for D-day was immense. The sky was overcast, clouds hung low in the sky, there was a strong south-west wind and heavy rain, the sea was

147

rough. The planners who had worked out all the details were frantic for there were only three days in the month when all the conditions for a successful landing were fulfilled, when the tides were right and the sky was moonlit.

The German weather forecasters predicted that the stormy weather would last for several days. The Allied meteorologists, however, believed that there would be an improvement for a few hours next morning. Thereupon the final decision was made; D-day was to be next day.

The 176,000 men crossed the Channel and landed on the coasts of Normandy. This was on June 6, 1944. Operation Overlord had begun.

I had begun to suspect the meaning of Operation Overlord three months previously. The strange expression recurred more and more often in the telegrams and documents that I photographed. I was the first person on the other side who knew about Operation Overlord.

I felt at the top of my form and went on with my espionage work recklessly and heedlessly, spurred on by the presence of Esra, my mistress, who stimulated my sense of adventure.

I explained Operation Overlord to her. I told her that it meant the second front demanded by the Russians. Whenever the Russians reiterated their demand, the phrase duly made its appearance in the telegrams. The second front was the only thing that Operation Overlord could mean.

I explained the great issues of the war to a girl of seventeen, who hung on my every word.

"The British want Turkey to intervene on their side be-

cause that would keep the Germans pretty occupied in the
Balkans, and the divisions they would have to keep in this
part of the world would not be available to resist the invasion of France. But Turkey is still unwilling to intervene.
Sir Hughe has telegraphed to London that it is prepared to
do so only after Operation Overlord has been a success."

I preened myself as a great strategist. Sitting in my arm-
chair with legs outstretched in my little rented house, I
dismissed Operation Overlord with a casual flick of my
hand.

"If the Germans keep their eyes open, they have nothing
to worry about," I said. "All they have to do is to take a
careful look at the documents I submit to them. There is
more and more emphasis on the phrase Operation Overlord. It won't be long now. If the Germans are clever, the
preparations they will make . . ."

Esra responded tenderly to my tirades. All memory of
the wild and passionate Mara faded from my mind. Esra
was gentle and timid and devoted. She behaved as if she
feared that her demonstrations of affection might annoy
me. Vainly and stupidly I took advantage of her love.

"Will you want to keep me with you always?" she asked.

The only thing in my mind was the sense of my own importance, and I was startled by her gentle question. I looked
at her angrily.

"You know yourself that one day we shall have to part,"
I said.

She accepted what I said, and only nodded.

I left her, and went to the British Embassy. I slept in my
room in the servants' quarters, and punctually at seven-

thirty A.M. took Sir Hughe his orange juice. While he was at lunch that day I photographed another document mentioning Operation Overlord.

Operation Overlord haunted me. Later I found out that it was I who first brought the phrase to the knowledge of the Germans. I went to the telephone and called up the German Embassy.

The contents of the documents led to the conclusion that an American General named Eisenhower was to be in supreme command of the operation. At the time the name meant nothing to me. Perhaps the fact that the Supreme Commander was to be an American was communicated to the Turkish Government in order to impress them. Perhaps it was thought that the Turks might regard an American Supreme Commander as a better guarantee of success, and perhaps the intention was to make it clear to them that it was now really high time for them to intervene. However, the reason why the name of Eisenhower cropped up in a document in connection with Operation Overlord was to me fundamentally a matter of complete indifference. All I cared about was having another opportunity of demonstrating my own importance.

The telephone was answered by Moyzisch's secretary, whom I did not suspect I had any reason to fear.

"Pierre speaking," I said.

I felt in fine form. I bellowed into the receiver as if I had another triumph to my credit. I made some cheaply flirtatious remarks.

"How are you, my dear?" I said. "Isn't it a wonderful

day? Spring will soon be here. What are you doing at Easter?"

"At Easter I'm going on leave," she answered dryly. "Who is speaking, by the way?"

"I'm Pierre, Moyzisch's best friend."

She giggled. "I want to know who you really are," she said. "All you ever say is just Pierre."

"Who I really am has nothing whatever to do with you, my dear. Now please put me through to Herr Moyzisch."

She said no more, I heard a click, and then Moyzisch was on the line.

"Let's have a game of bridge tomorrow," I said. "I've got a fistful of trumps already."

"All right, that's fine," he answered, but his voice sounded grumpy.

"Good heavens, what a bad mood you're in!" I said to him. "Please remember me to the charming young lady in your ante-room."

"Stop talking such rubbish," he muttered and put down the receiver.

We met at the corner of Ozdemir Street. We drove round the Old City as usual, and exchanged money and films.

"Your secretary told me she is going on leave at Easter," I said.

"Thank heaven," he muttered.

When I saw the disagreeable expression on his face, I grinned. Obviously he had nothing good to say about his secretary.

"I should like to take her out some time."

151

"If you like hysterical women, by all means do so," he grumbled.

That evening he was not in nearly such a good mood as I was. I patted him on the back, got out, and went back to my room in the servants' quarters. I put the money under the carpet, as I had used to do. I felt I could again afford to do so.

Easter, 1944, was a vital period in the life of Cornelia Kapp. I know that, now that it is all long since over and done with and the knowledge is completely useless to me.

At Easter seventeen years later I sat snugly in my Istanbul flat, trying to clear up the mystery of all the events of that time. A second tape-recording had just arrived by post. It contained more information from Seiler, the man with whose unsuspecting aid Cornelia had managed to become Moyzisch's secretary.

I listened to the tape, and found out how successfully she had deceived the Germans.

"What happened during the period immediately before Easter?"

"The girl seemed out of her mind. We didn't know why."

"What do you mean when you say she seemed out of her mind?"

"Her hysteria was sometimes practically intolerable."

"She says now that it was pure play-acting."

"I don't believe it. She was having a nervous breakdown."

"Perhaps she thought Moyzisch had started suspecting her."

"That may be, but actually she had nothing to worry about. We had no idea she was working for the other side. Every act of treachery that came to our notice sent her into a burst of fury."

"What sort of treachery?"

"At that time two Germans went over to the British. . . ."

"In Ankara?"

"No, in Istanbul. They were on the staff of the German Consulate-General—members of the *Abwehr,* intelligence specialists."

"Important people, then?"

"Yes. It created a great commotion among the Germans. First one disappeared, and then the other. Three went over altogether."

"And Cornelia Kapp pretended to be indignant about it?"

"Yes, she denounced them as traitors. She talked about her two brothers who were serving on the eastern front. She said that traitors like these men who went over to the enemy stabbed our front-line soldiers in the back. She used all the phrases that one could possibly imagine in such circumstances. She talked about duty to one's country and the loyalty owed to men in the line by non-combatants, and she said that Germany was bound to win the war in spite of her enemies. She made a lot of tremendous speeches on those lines."

"To divert any possible suspicion from herself?"

"Obviously. She even came to the office with letters her brothers had written her and read them aloud to us."

"What sort of letters?"

"They were very moving. The kind of thing soldiers write when trying to make sense of the war they are engaged in. The kind of letters soldiers write who believe they are risking their lives for something worth while."

"And she read those letters to you?"

"Yes. Moyzisch said that she sat and wept over them. She had a fit of uncontrollable sobbing at her desk."

"I suppose even traitors have fits of doubt."

"How do we know what goes on in a human being at such a time? I make no judgment on her."

"But she was just acting a part to show that she was a particularly good German who came from a family of particularly good Germans."

"Obviously there can be no other explanation. She wanted to deceive us. In any case she was such a bundle of nerves that Moyzisch had enough of her. He wanted to get rid of her."

"So it wasn't she that wanted to go, but he that wanted to get rid of her?"

"The two things may have coincided. We, of course, had no idea that she had practically got what she wanted and believed herself to be in danger. Perhaps she thought Moyzisch was keeping her under observation. If that was what she thought, she was completely wrong. He simply had had enough of her. He went to Papen. . . ."

"Why?"

"They wanted to get rid of her gracefully. After all, her father was in the diplomatic service. The idea was to get him to say that he wanted his daughter to rejoin him. The excuse was that because of the state of her health she was unable to carry out her duties satisfactorily."

"So a letter was sent off to Herr Kapp in Sofia. . . ."

"No, in the meantime he had been transferred to Buda-

154

pest. We wrote to him there, without Cornelia's knowing anything about it."

"So the idea was that it should look as if her father wanted her back?"

"Yes. We wanted to spare the old gentleman's feelings. She was inattentive, she made too many mistakes in her work, and whenever they were pointed out to her she had one of her hysterical outbursts. She was a nuisance."

"Obviously she was inattentive in her work for Moyzisch because she was paying so much attention to her work for the other side."

I listened to the tape-recording and imagined the state of mind in which Cornelia Kapp must have been at that time. She had practically attained her objective, she suspected who Cicero was, and at the same time was half dead with fear of being found out by the Germans and executed.

The recording went on.

Seiler's voice said: "We were surprised and delighted when one day she came to us herself and asked for leave. She said she wanted to spend Easter with her father in Budapest. Moyzisch promptly came and told me this, rubbing his hands with glee. He said that things were going more easily than we had expected. Cornelia was going on leave, and he would see to it that she didn't come back."

"So he just thought he was getting rid of a hysterical secretary in an easy and convenient manner?"

"Yes, and after that he was particularly friendly to her. I remember that one day he actually went shopping with her. She wanted to buy some Easter presents for her parents, as well as some things for herself."

"Did she go with Moyzisch to the A.B.C., for instance?"

"Yes, because that was the best shop."

I switched off the tape-recorder. So it *was* Cornelia whom I had met that day at the A.B.C.

I had wanted to give Esra a pleasant surprise. That day we had stopped and looked at the windows of the A.B.C.

"Oh, how lovely!" she had exclaimed, gazing entranced at a dress, a beautiful dress in which she would look like a lady.

That evening I sat in my servant's room, thinking about Esra. I remembered the dress, and imagined how delighted she would be if I took her one of those A.B.C. flat cardboard boxes and she opened it and found the dress inside.

The A.B.C. is one of the most fashionable stores on the Atatürk Boulevard—ladies' and gentlemen's clothing, suits made to measure. If I had been seen there by a member of the British Embassy, the game would have been up. How could I afford to shop at such an expensive place? They had known for a long time that they had a traitor in their midst, but they did not know that it was I. The thrill of playing with danger held me in its grip.

All that was necessary was to put my hand under the carpet, where the bank-notes were laid out.

I was filled with pride at being able to fulfil her wishes at any time, no matter what the cost. I had reached my peak, though I did not know it. I did not at that moment fear the slippery slope on the other side. I thought that things would go on like this for ever. I did not call myself to account, and laid all doubts aside. Whenever I felt misgivings I laid my hands on the money, felt it, held whole bundles of notes in my hands, and recovered my self-confidence. I was insatiable. Would this ever come to an end? I did not believe it. One day there would be an end of Cicero, the spy, and of Elyesa, the *kavass*, but that would merely mean the beginning of life for Bazna, the gentleman. I was a wealthy man.

I was enormously wealthy, no matter in what currency I worked it out. On that cold, clear, early spring morning I owned a fortune. I had £2,300,000 Turkish, or £300,000 sterling. It made me dizzy to think about it.

When I walked into the A.B.C. I saw Moyzisch. He looked right through me, his face expressionless, but I could see in his eyes that he was cursing my recklessness and cordially wishing me in hell. I was not interested in him, but in the attractive girl to whom he was acting as escort. I noticed her blonde hair, her long legs, her eyes—the restless eyes of a woman with a great thirst for life.

They were having difficulties in making themselves understood.

"May I act as your interpreter?" I said.

I asked the question with a smile, without suspecting that it was my enemy to whom I was offering assistance. I spoke to her in French, and explained to the saleswoman what kind of underwear she wanted. Moyzisch stood sullenly to one side while Cornelia and I chatted lightheartedly.

"I gather that you require underwear, madam. Won't you please tell me your measurements?"

We both found the situation very amusing. For weeks we had been mortal enemies, and now, without suspecting each other's identity, we engaged in a cheerful conversation.

157

"Are you German?"

"Yes."

"I hope you like it here in Ankara."

"Yes, I like it very much."

How was I to know that Cornelia had at that time long been sure where the spy Cicero was to be sought? She had nearly attained her objective. She knew that Cicero was a Turkish employee of the British Embassy. Once she had actually seen me, but she did not recognise me now.

Later I read her own words.

She too remembered our single meeting at the A.B.C. She wrote: "I well remember the man who helped me in such friendly fashion in choosing underwear at that store. I certainly did not recognise him as Cicero. He was very amusing to talk to. . . . I did not know what Cicero looked like," she went on. "One night he went to Moyzisch's rooms. I kept watch in front of the house, and I saw him in the distance, but it was too dark. He went off quickly in the direction of the tool-shed in the garden, and by the time I reached the spot he had vanished."

So she had kept watch on Moyzisch, had read the mail that came by courier from Berlin, had waited in the night, had systematically drawn the ring tighter around Cicero, in order to destroy him. And now, without knowing it, she was talking to Cicero.

"Thank you for your very kind help, *monsieur*," she said, and I smiled at her as she walked away with Moyzisch.

"*Au revoir, madame.*"

I decided that the next time I saw Moyzisch I should question him about this attractive creature, whom I supposed to be a girl-friend of his.

"The dress in the window, please," I said to the sales-woman.

Then I left the A.B.C. with my present for Esra under my arm and went to the Ankara Palace lounge. I looked at myself in the innumerable mirrors. I was well dressed. I now know that the perfume I then used was too sweet. I could not resist the temptation of flashing the diamond ring I had on my finger, so that I could see it in a mirror. I thought of the strange woman I had seen at the A.B.C. and I smiled at myself. I also thought about Esra, for whom I had just bought the dress. It was an expensive dress, but I could afford it. I felt intolerably pleased with myself. And once more I dreamed about the luxury hotel that I was going to build at Bursa.

I was smiling at my reflection with especial complacency —a smartly dressed gentleman, in a setting to which he belonged—when I saw the young woman again.

I saw her in a mirror as she entered the lounge. I was about to rise and go over to her and say: "Hello, *madame*, I had the pleasure of meeting you just now at the A.B.C.," but instead I sank back into the chair, staring at the mirror, incapable of moving. She was not alone. A young man had walked into the lounge behind her and was now walking by her side, talking to her familiarly. They smiled at each other, walked past me without seeing me, and disappeared into the restaurant.

Fear struck me like a blow. I tried to persuade myself that I had made a mistake, that I had been seeing ghosts, as had happened to me a few weeks before. But the fear would not leave me.

I remembered the young, smooth face I had seen on the

night of that furious chase in Moyzisch's car, the face I had seen flash past me after I jumped out. I had forgotten to think about that face and the threat that it meant to me. Now the threat had returned, and with it the fear.

The man who walked through the lounge with the young woman was the man with the young, smooth face.

Esra flung her arms round my neck. "Leave me alone!" I yelled at her, and pushed her away.

She looked at me like a whipped dog, discouraged and helpless.

"I only wanted to thank you. . . ."

"What for?"

My thoughts were miles away.

"For the dress you bought me."

I had forgotten all about it. Had I really brought it home for her? No doubt I had left it under the mirror in the hall.

"Never mind, it doesn't matter."

A thousand thoughts I could not get rid of were buzzing in my mind.

"Is anything the matter?" Esra asked. "Can I help you?"

Esra's tiny voice came to me as if from a great distance. My nerves failed me, and I shouted at her: "What's the matter? You've got the dress! What more do you want? For God's sake leave me in peace!"

She sat there, small and intimidated, with tears in her eyes.

"I only wanted to help you," she whispered.

"Stop being so goody-goody, no one can help me!" I shouted.

She crept away into a corner, sat down in a chair, and gazed at me, trying to understand.

"Don't stare at me like that!" I yelled at her. "Get out of here!"

The fear inside me made me rage with fury. I could have hit Esra because of her stupid ignorance and innocence.

"It was your fault I went into that damned store!" I shouted after her as she fled from the room. As if it would have made any difference if I had not gone to the A.B.C.

I felt I was stifling. Who was this man? Who was this young woman?

I had asked the hall porter at the Ankara Palace.

"Do you know the lady who just came in?" I said to him.

He shrugged his shoulders.

"And the gentleman?"

"He often comes here. He's an Englishman, I think. I think his name is Sears or something of the sort."

What did it matter what his name was? If he was a British agent it was certain that his name was not Sears, but something quite different, and in any case it did not make the slightest difference what his name was.

What mattered was that a German girl with whom Moyzisch went shopping was associating with an Englishman, and that the latter had once given chase to me. That was what mattered.

I tried to get Moyzisch on the telephone, but he was not in the Embassy. I could not get rid of my fear. My thoughts went round in circles.

Everything was possible. Perhaps the girl was a German agent. Why shouldn't she be? A confidential agent of Moyzisch's. Perhaps it was her mission to gain the Englishman's confidence. Perhaps Moyzisch had found out during the past few weeks who our pursuer was. It was possible. He would have no need to tell me this. There were a great many things which he kept from me.

Another possibility was that the Englishman was trying to gain the girl's confidence. Perhaps she was a girl-friend of Moyzisch's, and the Englishman was using her to keep his eye on him.

Another possibility was that the Englishman was on my trail and had seen me talking to the girl at the A.B.C. and had now joined her to find out whether she knew me. But in that case he would have been more likely to follow me. Or was it by pure chance that the two of them had come to the Ankara Palace together? Or, or . . .

There were no answers to these senseless questions.

Again I tried to telephone Moyzisch, but still he was not there.

Why was I afraid? Perhaps I had made a mistake, perhaps I only imagined that this man had been my pursuer. I tried to stifle the thoughts that tormented me, but did not succeed.

I went to the British Embassy, took the money from under the carpet and the camera, and went to my house.

I lay awake all night. I had no proof whatever that a threat lay over me, but deep inside me I felt certain that now I was really in danger, perhaps for the first time.

At four A.M. I got out of bed. I had no need to count my money, because I knew how much it was. I was a rich man, and I wanted to remain rich.

I destroyed all traces of my spying activity. I smashed the Leica into little bits and threw them into the Incesu

Deresi, which is a small river. The metal rods that for a long time I had given up using as a "tripod" went the same way.

Weeks previously I had hired a bank deposit safe, and had already put the greater part of the money in it. The remainder I put in a suitcase.

I woke Esra.

"Don't ask me any questions now," I said. "I want you to come to the British Embassy at midday today with this suitcase. I want you to wait in a taxi two hundred yards away. . . ."

I saw her anxious eyes, but had no time for explanations.

"Then we'll take the suitcase to the bank. In the meantime I want you to pack everything that belongs to me. Afterwards you will not come back here. . . ."

"Where am I to go?"

She tried to remain calm, but her whole body was trembling.

"You must take a room in a hotel. I'll settle up everything connected with the house. Then we'll see."

She swallowed.

Her hands clung to mine.

I stroked her. Since making up my mind I had grown calmer.

"Nothing has happened, but I'm packing up," I said. "I don't want to go on any longer."

I left her alone. At seven o'clock I was in my room in the servants' quarters at the Embassy. I removed the 100-watt bulb from the lamp on the bedside table and put a weaker one in its place. I wanted to overlook nothing. I took the 100-watt bulb down to the basement where the central heating apparatus was, and smashed it in the rubbish bin. Even if they suspected me a hundred times, they would not find a trace of evidence. There was nothing in my possession that an ordinary *kavass* would not be expected to possess.

I went down to the kitchen and filled a glass with orange juice. It was half-past seven, time to wake Sir Hughe.

I felt a tremendous sense of relief. A load was off my mind. I had the feeling that I had stopped at just the right moment.

I decided to stay on in the Embassy for a short time. It would be an enormous satisfaction to pretend to be nothing but a humble *kavass*, though in reality I had no need to be a *kavass*, a fact which nobody suspected. Then I should hand in my notice.

CHAPTER 9

I stole a glance at Sir Hughe. He looked peevish and pathetic, as he always did first thing in the morning before he had had his bath. I had grown used to it, and it calmed my nerves.

I had no need to tell him his bath was ready; my appearance in the bedroom was enough.

"Which suit, Your Excellency?"

He looked at the wardrobe, which I had opened, and after brief consideration pointed to a dark grey pin-stripe. I envied him his wardrobe. Still without speaking, he made his way to the bathroom, and I watched him. I am short and thickset, and have a hard, ugly face. I visualised myself in the lounge of the Ankara Palace in my smartest suit, and I felt crushingly aware of how cheap I must look, pretending to be a gentleman, not fit for polite society.

Sir Hughe was a gentleman even when he disappeared into the bathroom first thing in the morning, sleepy and unshaven.

I laid out his suit. I knew the shirt, the tie, the socks that went with it. I knew Sir Hughe's taste by now, and mistook that for having taste myself. For a moment that morning

my deficiencies were very clear to me. Envy was like a
poison I could not get out of my system.

Sir Hughe came back looking neat, clean, fresh, radiant,
confident and self-assured.

I, his deft, self-effacing, inconspicuous servant, handed
him his clothes as usual. Just for the sake of robbing him of
his appalling self-confidence, for which I envied him, I felt
like yelling in his face that I was Cicero.

He had washed away his pathetic, peevish, early morning
look, and he was cheerful and ready for the day's work.

"You're lucky to be with me," he said with a dry laugh,
as if he were amused at the idea.

I knew by experience that he did not want an answer. He
only wanted to talk, to show he was in a good humour; he
only wanted to say something cheerful to a member of the
staff.

"If you were with my colleague Papen you wouldn't have
anything to laugh about at the moment."

I started. I was glad that I was behind his back, and
began energetically brushing his jacket.

"Three Germans have deserted in Istanbul."

This was common knowledge; it was known to everybody
in all the embassies, from the senior diplomatist to the hall
porter.

"The rats are leaving the sinking ship, Your Excellency,"
I permitted myself to mutter.

"My colleague Papen now has another loss to complain
of." There was a trace of self-satisfaction in his voice.

How was it that I was suddenly aware that he was going
to tell me that a woman had now disappeared from the
German Embassy? Why could I think of nothing but the

girl whom I had seen with Moyzisch at the A.B.C.? I avoided letting Sir Hughe see my face. I went over to the chest-of-drawers and fetched him a clean handkerchief, which he arranged carefully in his breast pocket.

"A German woman member of the staff is missing," he said, again with a note of satisfaction in his voice. "The whole Papen household is upside down."

He had finished dressing. He looked at himself in the mirror, gave me a friendly nod, and went off to breakfast.

I had lost control of the situation and felt sick with uncertainty. What had happened? At the A.B.C. I had run into Moyzisch with a harmless-looking, attractive blonde, with whom I had laughed and joked, and then I had seen her again in the lounge of the Ankara Palace, in the company of a man with a young, smooth face whom I had every reason to fear. I could not have sworn that his was the face of our pursuer on the night of that wild car chase; on the other hand, if my eyes were to be trusted, I could have no real doubt that it was he. And now Sir Hughe had casually mentioned the disappearance of a woman from the German Embassy. What reason was there to connect her with the young woman I had seen at the A.B.C.? The whole thing might have been the product of my over-heated imagination.

Nothing had happened since the night when I destroyed everything that might have connected me with Cicero. Since then a week had passed, the Easter week of 1944. It was the fact that nothing whatever had happened that seemed to me to be so unnatural and got on my nerves.

I had given notice to the owner of the little house that,

with a mixture of irony and pride, I had called Villa Cicero, and my mistress Esra had moved to a little room in the Old City, where I had also taken two suitcases containing my made-to-measure suits, my expensive underwear, and my smart shoes. My money was in a safe at the bank, and the smashed Leica and the metal rods I had used for a "tripod" were at the bottom of the river. Had I acted precipitately, out of panic? Were my fears unfounded?

Sir Hughe—a gentleman living in a world infinitely remote from that of his servants—treated me with his usual friendly indifference. Sometimes I thought that his wife, whose alertness I had always feared, looked at me sharply. I assured myself that I was only imagining things. The only unusual feature in the situation was the fact that Moyzisch was unobtainable. I tried telephoning him again and again. But perhaps he was on a trip to Berlin; he had been to Berlin several months previously, and there was no reason why he should inform me that his superiors had sent for him.

While Sir Hughe was at breakfast I went down to the kitchen. Suddenly I found myself with an enormous amount of time on my hands. For months I had led a double life, as *kavass* and spy. Now it occurred to me that the amount of time I spent hanging about the house with nothing to do must seem highly suspicious.

Manoli Filoti, the chef, was only too delighted to have someone to talk to. He always welcomed an opportunity of passing on the latest gossip.

"Now a woman has deserted from the German Embassy," he told me with an air of great importance. There was nothing unusual in a member of an embassy domestic staff knowing such things. Turkish nationals were employed in all the embassies in Ankara, whether friend or foe, and a lively traffic went on among them. Turkish employees at the German Embassy exchanged Rhine wine or Moselle for whisky from the American or British or vodka from the Soviet Embassies. The embassy ladies and gentlemen drank the wine or the whisky or the vodka and could imagine where it came from, but did not ask inconvenient questions; and the latest gossip and rumours circulated by the same route as the whisky, the wine and the vodka.

"So I've heard," I muttered.

"Do you know who she is?" Manoli asked.

I shook my head.

He smiled with satisfaction at being able to tell me something.

"She's a secretary named Cornelia Kapp," he said.

This was the first time I had heard the name, and it did not yet mean anything to me. It was not necessarily the name of the young woman I had seen chatting familiarly to the man whose face I feared, and yet I had a foreboding of danger.

During the afternoon I served tea in Sir Hughe's room. Mr. Busk, his First Secretary, was with him.

When I walked in with the tray in my hand I heard the end of a sentence spoken by Mr. Busk.

". . . flown to Cairo. She is being thoroughly interrogated."

When I walked in Mr. Busk fell silent. Silently I laid down the tray, poured out the tea, put the plate of biscuits on the table and walked out of the room.

My head was in a whirl. What I had heard Mr. Busk

say might, of course, mean nothing at all, but it fitted in with the picture in my mind. I became certain that the young woman I had seen in the A.B.C. was Cornelia Kapp, that she was connected with Moyzisch, and might be in a position to know that Cicero was the British Ambassador's valet; and that it was Cornelia Kapp who was now being thoroughly interrogated in Cairo. I had the over-sharp sensibilities of a man whose life is in danger. I was certain that all this was not a figment of my imagination, and no doubt was left in my mind.

The next thing that happened was that I saw the man with the young, smooth face again.

He was standing in Ahmet Agaoglu Street, where the staff and tradesmen's entrance of the British Embassy is. Did that mean that they knew that Cicero worked in the British Embassy and was one of those who used the back door? The hall porter at the Ankara Palace had said that the man's name was Sears or something of the sort. His name was a matter of indifference to me, and I never found out what it was. For me he remained Sears-or-something-of-the-sort.

I did not know how long he had been waiting. He stayed there for an hour after I first noticed him. Then he walked away. He sauntered off slowly and apparently thoughtfully in the direction of the city. I hurriedly put on my coat and followed him. I remained a safe distance behind him. I did not care what Sir Hughe might think if he sent for me and found I was out.

Sears walked on like someone out for an evening stroll. He did not hurry, and did not look round.

In the Atatürk Boulevard he got into a taxi. As soon as

it drove off I dashed to the rank, jumped into the next wait-ing taxi, panting and out of breath, and told the driver to follow. The note I pressed into his hand made him very willing to do so.

This time the roles were reversed, and it was I who was in pursuit of the man with the young, smooth face. But on this occasion the chase was less dramatic; he did not know there was someone behind him whom there was any need to shake off.

We turned into the Marmara Sokagi. Sears' taxi stopped in front of a block of flats in a side-street.

"Drive straight past," I told my driver.

I saw Sears pay his fare, get out, and go inside.

I told my driver to stop and wait for me at the next corner.

I got out, accepting the risk that Sears might have seen me.

What had I to lose? If he already knew me, it would make no difference. If he did not, he would not notice me.

I went into the house and looked at the name-plates on the doors. Many foreigners lived there. It was a modern block of flats, of the kind popular with Embassy staff and businessmen. I did not see the name Sears, but there were plenty of names indicating Britons or Americans.

I had noticed Sears take a bunch of keys from his pocket as he walked into the building, so he evidently lived here.

So the situation was that he knew where to look for me and I knew where to find him.

I got into the waiting taxi and told the driver to put me down near the Embassy. No one had missed me.

I spent all my free time watching that block of flats, but

Sears, or whatever his name was, did not appear again. I had plenty of time to think. I worked out my chances. What could Cornelia Kapp know? What could she tell the British in Cairo? Supposing she told them that Cicero was Sir Hughe's valet? That was sheer supposition, and there was no proof. What would the British do? They could search my room, but I had got rid of everything suspicious; I had even smashed the 100-watt bulb. They would find nothing. They might keep me under observation, but I was positive they were doing nothing of the sort. Would I not have noticed it? I went daily to the side-street in the Marmara Sokagi, and made sure that if anyone had been following me I should have noticed it. But nothing happened.

I decided that all I could do was to stick it out, and in the end suspicion of me would fade. It was all a question of keeping my nerve.

To be able to live in peace as a rich man in the immediate future all I needed to do now was to keep my nerve for a little while longer.

Then I saw Sears again.

He was coming from the Tuna Caddesi, and there was a girl with him. She was in the uniform of the British W.R.N.S., and had short, black hair.

I was standing in a doorway, and my attention was concentrated on Sears, not on the girl. Not till they entered the block of flats did my nerves give the alarm signal.

I had watched Cornelia Kapp walking away after our conversation in the A.B.C., and I had watched her walking away after she had passed me with Sears in the Ankara

Palace. She had long fair hair, and this girl had short, black hair. But her gait, the way she held herself, the way she walked by Sears' side talking to him familiarly, enabled me to penetrate the disguise. The woman in British uniform was Cornelia Kapp.

Next day I at last got in touch with Moyzisch, and we met the same evening. I entered the German Embassy grounds as usual through the gap in the fence and walked past the tool-shed. Moyzisch was waiting for me at the entrance to the building in which his office was. We were alone. It was an hour before midnight.

He looked ill. There was no trace of his usual liveliness, and his face was twitching.

"Haven't you been in Ankara lately?"

"No, I've been away on duty."

He tried to make his voice sound normal, but there was no concealing his nervousness.

"I am not going on working for you," I said slowly.

"No doubt you have your reasons," he muttered, looking at me expressionlessly.

"There was a woman with you when I ran into you in the A.B.C.," I said. "What does she know about me?"

He stared at me, but said nothing.

"Could she be dangerous to me?"

He emerged from his brown study, and said hoarsely:

"She can't know anything."

I looked hard at him.

"I know all about her. She has deserted, hasn't she? Her name is Cornelia Kapp."

He did not move, and his face had hardened into a mask.

"What do you know?" he asked in a completely toneless voice.

"Has Cornelia Kapp deserted, or hasn't she?"

"She has disappeared. We don't know where she is."

He spoke reluctantly, as if the words had to be dragged out of him. It was a painful admission for him to have to make.

"She was your secretary, wasn't she?"

He nodded.

"She used to put me through to you on the telephone."

He did not deny it.

"What do you know?" he repeated.

"She's with the British," I answered. "I can show you the house where you can find them."

He went on sitting stiffly in his chair. Then he laughed aloud. It was a nervous, bitter laugh.

"What can I do about it?" he said. "Am I to kidnap them? We are in a neutral country. If I run into her in the street, am I to drag her away by her hair?" He was on the point of a nervous breakdown.

I did not change my expression. I said mockingly:

"She's no longer a blonde. She's now a brunette, and she's had her hair cut too short for you to be able to drag her away by it. What does she know about Cicero?"

He clenched his fists.

"She can't know anything," he said again. The repetition betrayed his uncertainty.

"All she knows about Cicero is that there is such a person," he said quietly.

"I hope so," I said, but I was unconvinced.

"I can give you the address where she is," I said.

174

I wrote down for him the address of the block of flats near the Marmara Sokagi.

"She's there with the young man who chased us that time," I said. "It looks as if he's more than just a friend."

He had nothing to say to this. We remained silent, until the silence became intolerable.

"There is still some money due to me," I said slowly.

He rose, as if it cost him a great effort, took a bundle of notes from the safe, and handed them to me.

"All right?" he said.

I took the money and walked towards the door.

"We shall not see each other again," I said. He acknowledged this silently.

I looked at him. He was biting his lower lip. He would not find it easy explaining away Cornelia Kapp in Berlin.

"*Au revoir, monsieur*," I said.

This was my last visit to the German Embassy.

What had happened since I had seen Moyzisch with Cornelia Kapp in the A.B.C.? The question exercised me for years, and I did not find the answer until I listened to Seiler's tape-recording so many years later.

"When did Cornelia disappear?"

Seiler's voice answered: "On April 6, 1944."

"That was Easter, wasn't it?"

"It was on the Thursday before Good Friday. She said that she was going on leave to see her father in Budapest."

"So she said!"

"Yes. We did not know she was lying. I remember mentioning to Moyzisch that day that at last he was getting rid of her. He had been so dissatisfied with her. He laughed, and said he would make quite sure that she got into the train."

"He wanted to make quite sure?"

"No, he didn't mean it seriously, he was joking. He wanted to be nice to her, he didn't want her to suspect he was getting rid of her. He bought a ticket for her. . . ."

"And?"

"The train she was going to take left at about six in the evening, and Moyzisch arranged to meet her on the plat-form with her ticket. He wanted to say good-bye to her and wish her a good journey. When she didn't turn up he nearly had a nervous breakdown."

"Did he immediately suspect she had gone over to the other side, as those other Germans had done?"

"No, I don't think so. He thought something must have happened to her, or that she had been taken ill. She was always so hysterical, and she was often away from the office because she said she was ill."

"No doubt in order to be able to meet her lover in peace and quiet. That Sears, or whatever his name was."

"Maybe. I've no idea."

"Sears, who was really an American and not an English-man as everyone thought."

"That is something I know nothing whatever about."

"Cornelia has herself admitted that she did everything for love. She says she met her boy-friend from Cleveland again in Ankara. The great love affair of her life, she calls it. That can only have been the man whose most noticeable feature is said to have been his young, smooth face."

"I repeat that I know nothing whatever about all that. I know nothing whatever about her motives for working for the other side. It may have been for money, or it may have been for love, but that is known only to herself."

"Very well, then. So Moyzisch's suspicions were not aroused immediately?"

"He searched the station for her, and when he failed to find her he came to see me, and we went together to her flat."

"And of course she was not there either."

"When we got there we knew at once. The flat was empty. Someone in the building told us that she had left during the afternoon with all her belongings. From that moment we assumed the worst."

"You mean that she had gone over to the other side."

"Yes."

"What did you do about it?"

"It had nothing to do with me. It was Moyzisch's business."

"And what did Moyzisch do?"

"He reported to Herr von Papen. What else could he do? For a time we thought she might have done something to herself."

"Was she a suicidal type?"

"Suicide was a possibility that we couldn't exclude. After all, she was a specialist in nervous breakdowns. For a time we refused really to believe that she had gone over to the other side. That might have had most unpleasant consequences for Moyzisch."

"Obviously. Didn't he report the matter at once to Berlin?"

"Of course he did. He had to, to avoid coming under suspicion himself. Berlin bombarded us with questions; they refused to believe in the possibility of accident or suicide, and immediately suspected desertion. Then Kaltenbrunner ordered Moyzisch to report to Berlin. Moyzisch suspected the worst."

"You mean that he might be arrested for negligence?"

"He had to be prepared for anything. He went to Istanbul to pick up the courier aircraft, but then he was tipped off by a friend, a man in the Foreign Ministry in Berlin, that it would be better not to come. He was advised to sham illness or something. In Berlin they were going to arrest him for allegedly aiding and abetting Cornelia's flight. They would have found plenty of excuses for venting their fury on him."

"So he didn't fly to Berlin?"

"No, he came back to Ankara. He was in a very bad way. Then Cicero turned up again and told him that Cornelia had gone over to the British—he thought the Sears character was British. Then we knew for certain."

The recording came to an end. Now I knew what must have been going on in Moyzisch's mind when I saw him for the last time. Cornelia's flight had put him in a position as dangerous as her own had been.

I also read what Cornelia said herself, writing from California.

"It had become too dangerous," she wrote. "I could no longer count on being able to work for the Americans without being caught. They had given me some poison to provide for all emergencies. If I had been arrested, I should not have lived to hear the death sentence, and I should never have fallen alive into the hangman's hands. I had obtained

the German diplomatic secret cipher for the Americans. I
had obtained copies of secret documents and handed them
over daily to my contact man. I had gained all the information about Cicero that it was possible to obtain. I knew
that he must be an employee of the British Embassy. I did
not wish to remain in danger any longer. I was convinced
that the information I had obtained was sufficient to establish which of the Embassy servants was Cicero. We took
advantage of the Easter holidays. Acting on American instructions, I applied for leave, on the ground that I wished
to visit my parents. It was arranged that the date of my
flight should be April 6. Moyzisch waited for me in vain at
the station; during the afternoon I had quietly packed and
left my flat with all my belongings. I went to the man I had
known since my Cleveland days, the man who was now
working for the American O.S.S. I was never paid for what
I did. My motive is to be sought in my relationship with
the young American whom I met again as an agent in
Ankara. But my chief motive was my desire to return to
America, and that was promised me as the reward for my
espionage work. Prior to that time the British had had no
suspicion of Cicero's existence. The American secret service
wanted to present their British colleagues with a *fait ac-
compli*. I was flown to Cairo and presented to the British,
and it was in Cairo that the British for the first time heard
the name of Cicero—from the Americans, who presented
me as the evidence. The British listened to everything with
expressionless faces. I have no idea whether they believed
me or not. For them it was a slap in the face, but they were
too proud to admit it. The British still minimise the whole
thing, to avoid losing face. Then I was flown back to An-

kara. My appearance was completely changed. My hair was cut short and dyed black, and I was put in the uniform of the British W.R.N.S. I would not have recognised myself. . . ."

But at the time I was completely in the dark, and there were no tape-recordings or letters from California to explain the situation. I continued to be the *kavass* of His Excellency the British Ambassador, expecting to be arrested at any moment.

But nothing happened to indicate that they had any suspicion of Cicero's identity. Life in the Embassy took its usual course. Did I only imagine that Sir Hughe was more reserved than usual? I had the impression that his attitude, not only to me, but also to Mustafa and Manoli Filoti and the butler Zeki, had changed somewhat. Perhaps he suspected all of us, but did not yet know which of us was the traitor.

I was haunted by fear. Sometimes it grew so intolerable that I decided to make an end of it. Every night in my little room in the servants' quarters I made up my mind to flee, and every night I got the better of my fear, because flight would have given them the last certainty—if it was not already in their hands.

I waited for the outcome, which looked as if it would never come.

CHAPTER **10**

I became aware of changes going on all round me. Ameri‚
cans appeared in the Embassy more often than usual. They
had discussions behind closed doors, and then they went
away again. What was the meaning of their frequent visits?
Who were they? Diplomatists? Agents? I was consumed
with curiosity and anxiety.

There was also a revival of comings and goings between
the British and the Turks. For months relations between
them had been strained, but now they grew close again.
Cornelia Kapp had vanished from the German Embassy on
April 6, and almost at the same time I had ceased my activities as Cicero and covered my tracks.

Was it not remarkable that, just at the moment when
relations between the British and the Turks grew closer,
those between the Turkish Government and the German
Embassy grew noticeably cooler? What was going on behind the scenes?

My imagination, stimulated by fear, suggested connections which were perhaps entirely imaginary. The urge to
know the real facts was almost overwhelming. Should I try
to have another peep at secret documents? Having suc-

ceeded so often, why not do so again? This time I had no intention of working for the Germans, but wished purely to satisfy my own curiosity, to calm my nerves. But I no longer had the courage to pry into secret files, telegrams and memoranda.

For months I had known what was going on behind the scenes. Now I felt that mysterious things were in progress, and sometimes I had to make a violent effort to prevent myself from trying to find out what they were. Sometimes I felt sure that traps were being laid for Cicero, and sometimes I thought that I had deliberately blindfolded myself to prevent myself from seeing the abyss towards which I was marching.

I did not know what was going on, and I did not know what to do. I realised that I no longer possessed the instinct which had hitherto guided me.

I had grown helpless, and all I could do was wait.

Germany was the biggest importer of Turkish chrome, and during the war Turkey was the only source of this raw material so vital to the German armament industry; and supplies had continued in spite of vigorous Allied attempts to stop them.

Mr. Busk, the First Secretary, now suddenly resumed his frequent visits to the appropriate Turkish Government departments, and high officials of the Turkish Foreign and Trade Ministries called frequently on Sir Hughe; and then, on April 20, Turkey stopped exporting chrome to Germany.

This was a serious blow to the German war machine, a slap in the face for Herr von Papen, and a triumph for Sir Hughe, who was unable to conceal his satisfaction.

That day he put on his diplomatic uniform to call on the

Prime Minister for the first time for a long time, and he was radiant when I helped him on with it.

The situation had changed, and Turkish neutrality was no longer assured.

If the country whose citizen I was was now falling completely into line with the British, that made my peril all the greater. As a Turkish citizen all I had feared hitherto was an illegal act of "revenge" by the British secret service if it found me out. But now it seemed possible that the British might officially ask the Turkish Government to punish me.

I was an insignificant nobody and, if I stood in the way of amicable Turco-British relations, the Turkish Government would not show much regard for my person.

I decided that I could no longer afford to wait and see whether the search for Cicero would one day be abandoned. I decided to leave the Embassy before it was too late. But it would never do to run away. I decided I must pluck up courage and leave in the simplest and most straightforward manner, i.e., hand in my notice, even if by so doing I risked attracting suspicion to myself.

Before taking the plunge I hesitated. Was this perhaps what they were waiting for? Would they prevent me from leaving the Embassy?

When I handed Sir Hughe his diplomatic jacket I felt my hands trembling. In his magnificent uniform he seemed the very embodiment of power against which I was utterly helpless.

"Your Excellency, there is something I should like to mention to you," I said.

183

I found it difficult to make my voice sound normal. There were beads of sweat on my brow.

"What is it?"

He was just going to see the Prime Minister, and he had no time for his *kavass*.

"Your Excellency," I said, "my wife is living in Istanbul with my four children. . . ."

I hesitated. What I said sounded false and unconvincing. The thought flashed through my mind that I had not bothered my head about my wife and children for months. I had banished all thought of them from my mind. My wife no longer meant anything to me, but now I was using her as an excuse.

"Well, what is it?" Sir Hughe said impatiently. He looked at me, coolly and indifferently. Was his indifference genuine or assumed?

"Your Excellency, I wish to give notice. I have a job waiting for me in Istanbul. My family . . ."

I did not dare look Sir Hughe in the face. I fetched the hat that went with the uniform.

"So you want to leave."

I thought I noticed a brief hesitation in his voice. Did I only imagine it, or were his eyes suddenly fixed on me searchingly?

"Your Excellency, I apologise for troubling you with my personal affairs. . . ."

I started stammering. My hands were damp with perspiration. I felt that submitting to his gaze was a last ordeal to which I must submit before I was safe.

He half turned away.

"Give it to me," he said.

184

I did not understand what he meant. My mind was elsewhere. He took a step towards me, and took from me the hat that I was clutching.

"I beg your pardon, Your Excellency," I muttered. Had I given myself away by my strange behaviour?

He stood there with his hat in his hands.

"You must know your own mind best," he said slowly. "Obviously, if you wish to leave, I shall put nothing in your way."

His voice was clear and controlled.

"Settle things with Zeki," he said.

He seemed suddenly to have lost all interest in me, and passed me over to the butler who was responsible for the domestic staff.

"Thank you, Your Excellency," I managed to stammer out.

I put my hand in my trousers pocket and took out a handkerchief, which I held in my clenched fist. When he looked away for a moment I wiped my hands with it.

For a moment he stood looking out of the window. Then he walked towards the door.

"Yes, settle things with Zeki," he said.

I hurried past him and held open the door, still with my handkerchief in my hand.

"Very good, Your Excellency," I said hurriedly.

I was glad when he walked out.

I walked out behind him and watched him walking away. Mustafa came down the passage, with a grin on his face.

"All dressed up," he said, indicating Sir Hughe with a movement of his head. Then he looked at me, and said: "Aren't you feeling well?"

"No, I'm not," I muttered, and wiped my forehead with the handkerchief. Something dropped. It was a key.

Mustafa grinned again.

"Look, you've dropped something. The key to Esra's flat?"

I was startled out of my life.

I had had the handkerchief in my hand in Sir Hughe's presence. If I had dropped the key in his presence, he would have recognised it, and the search for Cicero would have been over. It was the duplicate key to his black box.

I thought I had destroyed everything that might have incriminated me, but I had forgotten the two duplicate keys.

I quickly picked up the key that I had pulled from my pocket with the handkerchief without noticing it.

"Yes, it's Esra's key," I said hoarsely, and uttered a forced laugh.

How much longer would my luck hold?

I had had my chances in life and spoilt them, and I did not want to spoil this last chance of living a life of luxury.

Sometimes I wondered what other people thought of me —Sir Hughe, for instance. Did he think about me at all, or was I too insignificant?

Or what did Mr. Busk think of me? Mr. Busk, for whose benefit I had once written out details of my career—"born at Pristina on July 28, 1904. . . ." But what did that mean to him?

No doubt to him I was just a "native" from somewhere in the Balkans. Pristina? Never heard of it.

If they suspected me now, they obviously regarded me as venal and contemptible, and from their point of view, of course, they were perfectly right.

I had lost all connection with my family, from which I had kept away for many years. I was an outsider.

Sometimes I wondered how different my life would have been if I had kept to the prescribed paths. Now, for instance, while I packed my things in my servant's room, with my fear still alive within me, I wondered whether my future was really going to be so golden.

But at least I had seized the one great chance that had come to me in my life. A huge sum of money now lay in my name in a bank safe deposit.

I left the British Embassy on the last day of April, 1944. My departure could not have been more unobtrusive. I did not speak to Sir Hughe again.

He had given orders on the previous evening that the butler Zeki was to take over my duties for the time being. When I told Zeki that I would like to see Sir Hughe to say good-bye, that invariably haughty individual barely looked at me and said: "His Excellency has given instructions that he is not to be disturbed."

Were all my fears based on imagination? Need Cornelia Kapp's disappearance have meant the end of Cicero? Had I unnecessarily covered up my tracks? Need I have got rid of my camera and my metal rods and—though almost too late —the two duplicate keys which I threw into a canal?

For the last time I used the servants' entrance and found myself in Ahmet Agaoglu Street, with a cardboard attaché case in my hand. Nobody realised that Cicero was leaving the British Embassy.

Sir Hughe had not wished to be disturbed. I might have outwitted him, but that did not mean that he accepted me as an opponent.

What is the classic ending of a spy story? The spy is led out to where the execution squad is waiting, and treated with respect by his enemies. There is a roll of drums, and he speaks a few brave words before the order to fire is given.

But I walked down the empty street with my attaché case, unnoticed by anyone, a short, thickset man, beginning to grow bald.

At that moment I did not feel convinced of my own importance.

I rented a smart flat in the Maltepe quarter and lived the life of a wealthy idler. When Esra came to see me I enjoyed her company, and persuaded myself that she was an ideal mistress, more like a slave than a girl-friend. All the same, I realized that I was beginning to tire of her. When I was honest with myself I was forced to admit that this was be-cause she had known me as a *kavass*; she reminded me of something I wanted to forget.

"Would you like to go to the university? I'll pay," I said to her.

I spoke to her like a moralist dissuading a young girl from living the life of a kept mistress. However, she saw through my long speeches about the deeper meaning of life and the possibilities open to an educated young woman in modern Turkey, and realised what I really meant. She did not weep or make a scene. She had been brought up in the Muslim tradition, according to which all that is required of a woman is to bow to the inevitable.

I met a Greek singer named Aika. She had a first-class figure but a third-class voice. Aika was not good for very much, but she kept to the rules of the game. So long as I kept her, she was not unfaithful to me. She was blonde and had long legs, and reminded me of Cornelia Kapp, whom I blamed for having brought Cicero's career to a premature end. Might I not have grown even richer but for her? Might I not have caused my country to maintain its neutrality to the end? "You resemble a woman whom I hate," I said to Aika. She only laughed. Because I lavished money on her she listened patiently to my tirades, and her applause took the form of kisses.

So time passed, and I drifted on. Was this the life of which I had dreamed?

The invasion of Normandy took place on June 6. "Operation Overlord!" I exclaimed. "This is Operation Overlord!" Aika looked blank. "What's that?" she asked.

"That's what they call the invasion of Normandy, but those are things you don't understand. . . ."

"Shall we go to the Ankara Palace?" she said. She could be terribly indifferent to what was going on in the world.

Numan Menemencioglu, the Foreign Minister, resigned. He had always been friendly to the Germans, and the new Turkish policy meant that he could not continue.

The British now had their own way completely with the Turkish Government. The Turks forbade German shipping the use of Turkish waters, and on August 2 severed diplomatic relations with Germany. It was only a question of time before they declared war.

What had all this to do with me? Had I once imagined that I could hold up the course of events?

Quite suddenly Sir Hughe was withdrawn from his post. I learned later that on August 31 he received a telegram from Mr. Eden to that effect. He was given a week to leave the Embassy. Such haste was unusual, and it gave me food for thought.

He was appointed Ambassador to Brussels before he finally retired. The Foreign Office was trying to save face.

Once more I poked my nose into something that had nothing to do with me. I was present at Sir Hughe's departure.

Did I want to feel a sense of triumph? Did I want to set eyes once more on the man whom I had deceived and exploited to my own advantage?

When the car drew up outside the Embassy I was waiting in the street.

The British Government did not make any public statement about Cicero until six years later, after publication of L. C. Moyzisch's book *Operation Cicero*, when the awkward question was raised in the House of Commons.

Sir Hughe himself made only one public statement about Operation Cicero. In this he agreed that the story was substantially true, and said that the whole thing, or at any rate the part of it that mattered, had extended over a period of about six weeks. A few days after they had found out what was going on they had managed to put a stop to it. The valet's first name was Elias; Sir Hughe could not remember his surname. The man had of course been thoroughly screened before being employed in the Embassy, and Sir Hughe thought he had been working elsewhere in the Embassy before coming to him. After this affair the man had been sacked or sent away on leave. He had vanished, and no one knew what had become of him.

That is not quite correct. I did not vanish; when he left the Embassy Sir Hughe could have seen me standing outside in the street. His car drove up and he appeared in the doorway, a diplomatist who had learned to seem unruffled in all circumstances.

Did he make a better exit than mine? I left by the servants' entrance, and he walked out through the front door. I carried my own attaché case, while he had no need to bother about his luggage. I walked down the hill into the town, while he drove quietly away in his big car.

He sat erect against the cushions. I raised my hat, but he did not see me.

I soon became disillusioned with my new way of life. What did Aika's kisses, or her exclamations of pleasure when I bought things for her, mean to me? What did I get from the politeness with which I was treated by the waiters at the Ankara Palace because of the big tips I gave them?

I was good for nothing, I had learned nothing, and all I had was money. I called myself a business man, and went into the second-hand car trade. I still could not get away from cars.

I did my business in the lounge of the Ankara Palace, where I read the papers and cut out the advertisements of cars for sale.

One day I noticed an advertisement in which the advertiser gave his telephone number. I recognised it; it was that of the residence of Mr. Busk, the First Secretary of the British Embassy.

I had an irresistible urge to find out whether he knew I was Cicero. Or had the secret service and Sir Hughe restricted the circle of those who knew the truth in order to minimise the whole unflattering business?

I called at Mr. Busk's residence and announced that I was interested in the car advertised as being for sale.

Mr. Busk received me in his drawing-room. He stared at me, and I enjoyed the sense of my own impudence.

"So it's you, is it?" he exclaimed.

I bowed.

"Yes, sir. I'm a dealer in second-hand cars now, sir, and trade's quite brisk, I'm glad to say."

He made polite inquiries after my health, and I told him I was well.

Did he really know nothing, or was he play-acting?

I asked whether the car for sale was the one I remembered. He said it was, and I offered him £300 sterling for it.

He accepted. My smart suit seemed to annoy him.

"May I have another look at the car, sir?"

We went down to the garage, and I inspected the car. I had a good look at the tires, speedometer, and seats.

"It has been carefully looked after," I said.

Mr. Busk's expression did not change. It was a strange sensation to be doing a deal with him.

"How is that children's nurse whom you once had, sir?" I asked, and while he answered I lifted the bonnet.

"She met an American in London, and now she's in the United States."

I bent over the engine, and felt a certain disappointment at learning that Mara, the girl with the husky voice, evidently no longer missed me.

"Is she married?" I asked, closing the bonnet again.

"Married and has a child," Mr. Busk answered. It evidently gave him no pleasure to discuss a former servant with a former *kavass*.

"I'll take the car," I said, and paid him £300.

I had no desire to cheat him. I paid him with money the Germans had given me. I believed it to be genuine. How were Mr. Busk or I to know that the £5 notes I handed him were forged?

CHAPTER 11

I had believed myself to be in possession of unimaginable wealth, which I hoarded and squandered, because I had been a poor man for too long to be able to deal with it rationally and sensibly.

The story of my hoard of Bank of England notes was a strange one, and its roots lay in Turkey.

In the early stages of the war the Germans bought large quantities of Turkish linen because they were unable to produce linen of similar quality at home. The rags were manufactured into paper of the same type as that used for British bank-notes. That was the first step.

Then the concentration camps were combed for skilled printers, engravers and other specialists of all nationalities. They were put in a special section of the concentration camp of Oranienburg, where they were given preferential treatment and put to work turning the paper made of Turkish linen rags into replicas of British bank-notes.

By putting these into circulation in large quantities in neutral countries the Germans hoped to weaken, if not undermine, the pound sterling. Department VI of the *Reichssicherheitshauptamt*, to which Moyzisch belonged, found another use for them. As it was very short of genuine currency with which to pay its agents abroad, it rewarded the dangerous services performed by the latter in forged currency.

The Germans put their forgeries through a severe test before putting them into circulation. They sent an agent to Switzerland, where he presented a quantity of notes to a bank and said he would be very much obliged if they would examine them most carefully, as he had reason to suspect that some of them might not be genuine. The Swiss bank spent three days scrutinising them and subjecting them to all the usual tests, and ended by declaring them to be genuine. In order to leave no stone unturned the Swiss actually submitted the serial numbers, dates of issue, and signatures to the Bank of England, which confirmed that notes of the issues referred to were in circulation. Thus the forgeries passed this crucial test with flying colours.

At the end of February, 1945, when Turkey entered the war on the Allied side, deliveries of linen to Germany had long since ceased, but past deliveries had fulfilled their purpose.

In May, 1945, the alarm was sounded by the American secret service in Austria. It received information that peasants living in the River Traun area were fishing bank-notes out of the river in enormous quantities. The area was cordoned off, and the Americans started fishing for money. They ended by recovering about £20 millions.

The Americans found a former concentration camp inmate named Skala, who was most reluctant to talk because he feared that he might have been committing a grave penal offence in helping to forge the money, though he had

had no choice. However, his interrogation finally led to the conclusion that forged notes had been manufactured to the tune of about £150 millions.

When the Bank of England was informed of this it started quietly withdrawing from circulation all the notes of the series which the Germans had copied. Official silence was maintained because the British feared the effect of a public announcement on the international money market.

The Germans who had taken part in this gigantic fraud declared that forged notes to the value of 29 million Reichsmarks had been smuggled into Turkey, partly for the purpose of shaking the pound, partly to pay a German agent. This agent was Cicero, and Cicero was I.

The American secret service inquiries and the measures taken by the Bank of England remained secret. I did not suspect that the Germans had deceived me as grossly as I had deceived Sir Hughe.

The bank-notes that I hoarded so jealously were not worth even the price of the Turkish linen out of which they had been manufactured. Instead of possessing immeasurable wealth, I was a poor man without knowing it.

If I had kept a diary at that time, it would have read something like this:

The risks I took have been rewarded, and my efforts have been crowned with success. I have divorced my wife, but that was inevitable. I treated her, and the four children, generously, of course. I now live in a comfortable flat, of the kind of which I always dreamed. I am not such a contemptible individual, after all. My ex-mistress Esra is studying at the university at my expense. My ex-mistress Mara got

enough money out of me to seem a worth-while match to
an American. My ex-wife and the children are well. My
conscience is clear. The British, perhaps out of regard for
their ambassador's reputation, are taking no action against
me; the story that I would have to tell, if it were made public, would bring down too much ridicule on their heads. I
am rich and independent. My mistress Aika makes an excellent impression. She is taller than I am, but never mind,
with my money I out-top them all. The Germans have lost
the war, but that, after all, might have been foreseen. What
does it matter to me? Life goes on; above all, my life goes
on. I now live in Istanbul with Aika, my beautiful, expensive mistress, and we do a great deal of travelling. We have
been to Bursa, which is a lovely place, and there my dreams
will come true. I am going to build a hotel there, a hotel on
Swiss lines. It will be my hotel, a *rendezvous* of the fashionable world. Aika admires my vitality. "You are a great man,"
she says. I am not in love with her, but I can afford to be
seen anywhere with her. . . .

It would have been a very proud and personal diary, written in total ignorance of the truth.

I gave up the second-hand car trade. An Istanbul building contractor became interested in going into partnership
with me, and we founded the firm of Bazna and Oztemel.
I had impressive letter-headings printed, and the great contracting firm of Bazna & Co. was born.

Nobody asked where I came from, or where my money
came from, or how I used to earn my living. My appearance
was confident and self-assured. I smelt of expensive soap. I
had forgotten having ever been a *kavass*.

I obtained the Government contract for building the big

new parcel post office at Istanbul. The firm prospered, and I dined with important Government officials.

I was approached by the Bursa municipal authorities, who asked me to tender for the building of a new school. I employed architects and engineers to draw up plans, prepare models, calculate costs. I submitted my tender and got the contract. The school was built, and at the opening ceremony, which was attended by all the notables of the area, it was named the Hasim Iscam elementary school. The first contact with Bursa was established.

There was a very decent hotel there already, called the Celik. It had a good reputation, but was old-fashioned.

I decided that the best thing to do would be to come to terms with the proprietor. There were hot springs at Bursa, and all over the world people wanted to forget the war. The tourist trade would grow by leaps and bounds in the postwar world, Bursa was the best site in the whole of Turkey, and the thing to do was obviously to build a huge hotel there. Moreover, the best site in Bursa was next door to the Celik, and that was where we must build the most exclusive spa hotel in Turkey. We could call it the Celik Palace.

I grew very heated about this project, and quarrelled with my partner over it. It was too risky and speculative for him.

I parted from him and found a new partner, named Niyazi Acar. We made new plans and founded a new firm called Bazna & Acar, and this time it looked as if the Celik Palace was really going to be built. It was too big an undertaking to be practical without Government aid.

Aika, smiling, cool, and lovely, was my constant companion. I talked to her about my grandiose project.

"The ancient Roman emperors used to take the waters

here," I told her. "You know how people are; they like taking waters the healing qualities of which have been known
since antiquity. We shall have a summer season and a
winter season." Aika rattled the ice in her whisky glass.

I showed her round the town. The climate of Bursa is
unique. The peaches that grow in the fruit gardens there
weigh a pound each. Mount Uludag, which rises behind the
town, is nearly 8,000 feet high.

"It will be a paradise for skiers," I said.

I spread out in front of Aika the plans and sketches prepared by my architects.

"We shall build the hotel over one of the springs, so that
our guests will be able to take the waters without leaving
the premises. The hotel will be five stories high, and we shall
have 150 rooms with 200 beds, every room with its own
bathroom, telephone, and every imaginable comfort. The
lounge will be magnificent. I have a weakness for hotel
lounges. It's wonderful to sit in them and watch people."

My dream seemed to be on the point of coming true.
The beautiful and cool Aika stroked my hand and smiled.

Anxiety and alarm started spreading among the bankers,
businessmen, and public officials of Istanbul. Forged British bank-notes were circulating in the town, and such was
the prevailing nervousness that businessmen whose ac-
counts were settled in Bank of England notes got into the
habit of having them examined for genuineness.

The merchant Avadis was paid a large sum in sterling by
the merchant Ismail Karaali for a consignment of caustic
soda. A friend of Avadis's, named Burhan, who happened
to be making a business trip to Switzerland, took some of

199

the notes with him at Avadis's request to have them examined by a Swiss Bank. Once more the notes were subjected to every recognised test and, to make quite sure,
some of them were sent to the Bank of England. It was a
repeat performance of what had happened during the war,
when the Germans first tried out their forgeries.

But this time the result was different. The notes were denounced as forgeries.

When Burhan went back to Turkey he was arrested. He
gave the police the name of Avadis, who was arrested too;
and Avadis gave the name of Ismail Karaali as that of the
man who had made a payment with the forged money.

Karaali appeared before an examining magistrate. He,
Avadis, and Burhan were charged with putting forged notes
into circulation.

"Where did you get the money from?"

Ismail Karaali had no difficulty in remembering. He produced his account books and showed them to the examining magistrate. They demonstrated his connection with the
building of the Celik Palace which was then in progress at
Bursa with Government backing.

"So you claim to have got the money from a consortium
on which the Government is represented?"

The examining magistrate smelt a scandal. The biggest
hotel in Turkey's chief watering place, the future pride of
the Turkish tourist industry, an enterprise in which the
State itself was a shareholder, was being built with forged
money? The idea put Government officials in a panic.

I was living in a suite of rooms in a Bursa hotel. On the
evening when the end came I was sitting with two architects, discussing the appearance of the façade of the Celik

Palace. The ground floor was to be of red sandstone, and the four upper floors were to be grey-green.

I was called to the telephone.

The receiver was near the window. When I looked out I could see the building site. They had already got to what was to be the big dining-room on the first floor.

I picked up the receiver, and heard my partner's excited voice. He said the police had been to see him, and all hell was loose in Istanbul. I thought I had not heard him correctly, and asked him to repeat what he said.

He told me that the firm's assets had been confiscated.

My mind reeled, and refused to take in the devastating information.

"Was it you who paid Ismail Karaali in British banknotes? Was it you?"

"Of course. I don't understand . . ."

"The notes were forged."

The voice at the other end of the line grew incoherent. I could not make out what it said, and put back the receiver. Aika found me lying there an hour later; the architects had told her that I had collapsed. They did not know why, I had just collapsed, and lay there raving deliriously.

Aika asked me questions in a cool and matter-of-fact voice. I answered her, but I can no longer remember what I said.

When the delirium subsided I was completely calm, listless, and apathetic. Aika realised more clearly than I did the meaning of that telephone call. She left me the same evening.

Fortune smiled on no one involved in Operation Cicero.

After the breaking off of diplomatic relations with Turkey

the members of the German diplomatic mission were put in a kind of honourable internment. Eventually they were put on board the Swedish ship *Drotningholm,* and the end of the war overtook them while they were still in the Mediterranean. The *Drotningholm* put into the port of Liverpool, and the British arrested those passengers who were thought to be dangerous. Among them was Moyzisch.

He was kept for months in a camp for "enemy specialists" and was interrogated day and night to the point of exhaustion.

"Who was Cicero?"

"Is it correct that he was the British Ambassador's valet?"

"Do you know his real name?"

"Did you pay him with forged bank-notes?"

"We don't believe that you know nothing about the money having been forged. Tell us the truth. How much money did he get from you?"

"Tell us what he was like. We don't believe you don't know his real name. What was his name? Tell us his name. His name, his name, his name . . ."

He could not tell them what he did not know. Months later they let him go, a worn, emaciated man glad to be able to vanish into anonymity again.

He returned to his home in Austria. Seventeen years after our joint adventure I met him at Innsbruck. We smiled coolly, and each of us looked inquisitively at the other to see what life had done to him. We felt no particular sympathy for each other. Our great adventure had rewarded neither.

I have always wondered what I should say if I met Cornelia Kapp.

"Was it worth while?" I might ask her. "How much did the Americans pay you?"

But she did not do her work for dollars.

"I wanted to go to America," she has said. "The Americans promised to take me to America, and that is why I worked for them."

After she had been tracked down in America I had no need to go on wondering what her reward had been. She has said: "From Ankara I was taken by air to Washington by way of Cyprus and Britain. They put me in a camp. They seemed to know nothing about my services for the United States. I went through a terrible time. I was kept under observation and treated like a criminal. I was not even allowed to go to the toilet except under observation. I was subjected to terrible shock treatment of the kind that is given to the mentally ill. Then I was put in an ordinary prison in Washington, together with prostitutes. I felt terribly insulted after all I had done for America."

Then I read what Violet Kyle, otherwise Pinky, the waitress at the restaurant in Chicago, had to say.

"Cornelia came to us from a camp at Bismarck, North Dakota," she wrote. "She too worked as a waitress. We became friends. There was a German bar-tender named Wolfgang, I forget his surname, he too had been in a camp. He was very much in love with Cornelia. He gave her the address of Mr. Coutandin, who was of German origin. Cornelia became a tenant of the Coutandins. Wolfgang was sent back to Germany, but Cornelia never answered his letters. She used to drink twenty cups of coffee a day, and was a bundle of nerves. She told me that she loved her father above everything. He had spoiled her dreadfully. As a child she had always been given everything for which she asked. She never had much money here, but she shopped at the best and most expensive stores."

So, for a time, the torn, unhappy Cornelia lived in Chicago, with the Coutandins.

I also read what the Coutandins had to say.

"She told us all about Ankara. She had given the secret cipher and all the secret information to the Americans. She had to leave Ankara in April, 1944. She left it only reluctantly, because the night life there was so exciting and she had a great love affair there. We were sorry for Cornelia, but she turned out to be a strange girl. She talked continually about a young man, the love of her youth, whom she had met in Ankara. She did everything she could to find him again in America, until she eventually discovered that he was dead. She made the acquaintance of her husband here—he lived in our house too—and then they got married. In 1947, when she received the news of her father's death, she sobbed and shrieked: 'It's my fault: It was because of me!' She believed her father had died of grief because of her. The F.B.I. used to pay her visits once a week."

Was Operation Cicero not like a disease whose contagion of misfortune spread to all who came into contact with it?

CHAPTER **12**

I found a perverse consolation in not being the only one ill-treated by fate. I pounced greedily on every scrap of information I could gather about any of the others.

Ruth Coutandin, the daughter of the couple whose tenant Cornelia Kapp became, saw Cornelia in California. Her husband had obtained a job in southern California. Ruth Coutandin wrote: "They have a house not far from the Pacific Coast. It is a pretty little house, and Cornelia's children are clean and lively. She herself makes a calm impression, but can be infuriatingly obstinate. She is said to be a regular and enthusiastic attendant at Salvation Army meetings for alcoholics, and to do a great deal of good work in that connection. Visitors are struck by the fact that in every room in the house there are shields bearing the words 'God forgives all,' and that the words 'Believe and ye shall be saved' and 'God is Salvation' are framed in the lavatory."

My own house is in a little side-street remote from the metropolitan bustle of Istanbul. The Zulali Cesme Sokak is a rather steep, dirty, blind alley, and could not by any stretch of the imagination be called a smart residential

205

street. When I come home in the evening I have to climb steep stone steps to the second storey. The staircase is dark, and so is the doorway. Behind the door there is a very ordinary flat, with cosy easy chairs, and a cosy sofa, the background to a cosy family life. Father in his late forties, very fond of sweet coffee and sweet drinks, mother, and four children. When I look at myself in the mirror I try to see myself as the former great adventurer, the ruthless spy with glittering dreams. In reality all I see is a bald-headed, care-worn paterfamilias, living with his second wife, who is twenty years his junior. The four children of my previous marriage visit me at intervals.

An adventurer with eight children? The man who has been called the most dangerous spy of the Second World War? I am not very fond of looking at myself in the mirror. I no longer have any reason for vanity.

All that I have achieved is this cosy flat. Once upon a time there was a woman who admired me for my vitality—the smiling, cool and calculating Aika. But my vitality failed me.

It was destroyed in my battles with the police, with the forces of justice, with my creditors.

"You put forged bank-notes into circulation."

"I did not know they were forged."

"You tried to defraud people."

"I paid out the money in good faith. The defrauding was done by the Germans, not by me."

"How can you prove that?"

Years passed, but the questioning and interrogations and official suspicions remained the same.

I met Duriet, and she became my wife. She knew I was poor, but did not mind.

The courts finally gave up trying to stamp me as a criminal. But they insisted on my repaying the debts that I had contracted by unknowingly paying bills with forged money.

I gave singing lessons, because all I had left was my voice, which had once earned me compliments from Sir Hughe. The small fees I earned went to my creditors. I dealt in second-hand cars, and my creditors took their share of the profit. When I was at my wit's end I borrowed an evening dress, hired the Saray cinema in the Istiklal Caddesi, and had bills printed announcing a concert.

On the morning after the concert I read in the newspaper: "Placards in the street had made it known for several days past that a man named Elyesa Bazna was going to give a concert. The baritone Bazna last night sang arias by Handel, Giordani, Verdi, Mascagni, Grieg and Bizet. He ended by singing O *sole mio*.

"There was great applause after every song, though only a few hundred were present. The evening ended tragi-comically. Among the audience was an Istanbul merchant who was a creditor of the singer's, and he was accompanied by a bailiff who confiscated the takings before the concert ended."

I had made a public exhibition of myself, become a figure of fun. When I crept out of the cinema by the back door and walked home through the dark streets in evening dress, taking no notice of the people who stared after me, I felt a very lonely man.

Nothing was left for me but to try begging.

I went to the German Consulate-General, now known as the Consulate-General of the German Federal Republic. The Germans had already gone quite a long way towards getting back on their feet.

"I wish to speak to the Consul-General, please."

"In what connection?"

"A financial matter."

The Consulate-General was a handsome building, solidly furnished, and the officials were correct from head to foot and to the very depth of their souls.

They looked at me mistrustfully. My appearance was not very confidence-inspiring. My suit was shabby, and my face fallen in.

A junior official came and listened to what I had to say.

"I know nothing about the matter," he said. "We have no official knowledge here of any Operation Cicero."

What else was I to expect? Could Moyzisch have written me out a certificate saying: "Bazna, Elyesa, no special physical characteristics, carried out espionage on our behalf. We request all those concerned, particularly the British, to give him all possible aid and assistance in his arduous task"? I had no documents to show the consulate officials, and documents were the only thing of which they took any notice.

"I was grossly cheated by the German Reich. The Federal Republic is legal heir of the Reich, and I therefore have a claim against your Government."

I spoke quietly and hopelessly, there was no conviction in my voice, and I felt ashamed of myself, because the man to whom I was speaking regarded me merely as an importunate beggar.

"I'm afraid there's nothing I can do in the matter. I'm very sorry."

He was obviously sorry for me. He fiddled impatiently with the file in front of him, and made it evident that I was being a nuisance. The work that he wanted to get on with was certainly of great official importance, so I left.

There was no reason why I should not humiliate myself still further. I went to see Herr Jenke, Ribbentrop's brother-in-law.

He, like the other members of the German Embassy, had had to leave Turkey in the *Drotningholm*. For a time he lived at Baden-Baden, and eventually returned to Turkey at the end of 1949 or the beginning of 1950. He went back to the contracting business in which he had been engaged before his brother-in-law, the German Foreign Minister, persuaded him to join the German diplomatic service.

I wanted his help. I waited for a long time in the street, thinking over what to say to him. He knew that I had worked for the Germans, and that they had defrauded me; he might even be able to help me by a small loan.

I rang the bell and gave my name. I was asked to wait outside the door. I had to wait a long time.

Then a maid came and told me that Herr Jenke was very sorry he was unable to receive me.

Two days later he died.

He went sailing with some friends in the Sea of Marmora, and the boat overturned. It was just an accident. Everyone was rescued, but when Herr Jenke was pulled out of the water he was dead.

The newspapers called it a "mystery death," but the post-mortem showed that he died of heart failure as a result of shock.

So there could be no more applying to him for help.

One evening, feeling very depressed, I sat in my cosy arm-chair and drafted a letter. I addressed it to His Excellency Dr. Konrad Adenauer, Federal Chancellor, Bonn, Germany.

I thought very carefully about the phrasing of what I had

to say, and made a careful fair copy of my first rough draft.

"Your Excellency," I wrote, "the undersigned, Elyesa Bazna, herewith takes the liberty of submitting to Your Excellency the facts described below in the hope of securing Your Excellency's intervention in righting at least part of the great wrong that has been done to me. I was in the service of the German Embassy in Ankara, and during the war went over to the service of the British Embassy in Ankara out of pure sympathy for the German Reich in order to be able to render service to the latter. The great services that I rendered at the risk of my life, my freedom, my reputation and my livelihood were rewarded with forged British banknotes. . . ."

It was a long, detailed, servile letter, dictated by bitter need. It ended:

"For this reason I dare hope for an early and favourable reply to my request, and in conclusion I desire to express to Your Excellency my most sincere thanks and to ask Your Excellency to accept this expression of my particular regard and esteem."

Had I not in my own fashion conducted nightly conversations with the great ones of the world? Had I not obtained glimpses into the plans of Churchill, Stalin and Roosevelt? My letter to Dr. Adenauer for the last time gave me the feeling of being in contact with one of the world's leading men.

Months later I received a reply from the Foreign Ministry in Bonn. It said:

"In reply to your communication dated April 16, 1954, addressed to the Federal Chancellor, you are informed that the Foreign Ministry is investigating the matter referred to.

The Foreign Ministry will not fail in due course to communicate with you again."

The signature was illegible.

Four months passed before anything else happened. The letter that then came from Bonn was brief. It said:

"*Re* claim against German Reich. The Foreign Ministry regrets being unable to take any action in the matter referred to."

I am still alive.

I buy and sell. It is not for nothing that I am a Levantine. Levantines always land on their feet, though the floor their feet land on is not always covered with expensive carpets.

Last summer I went to Bursa with Duriet, my wife. We travelled by way of unpaved roads, by bus.

"It's wonderful here," Duriet said quietly.

I showed her the peach gardens, Mount Uludag, and the hot springs.

We entered the Celik Palace Hotel. It is a truly magnificent hotel. Two page-boys in light blue uniforms stood by the door and zealously opened it when guests approached.

We sat in deep, soft armchairs in the big, low lounge, looked at the palms growing in big tubs, watched the coming and going of the guests, and read the prospectuses lying on the little tables.

I read the hotel prospectus to Duriet.

"In summer our guests enjoy the magnificent surroundings and bubbling springs and the woods round Bursa. In winter the slopes of the majestic Mount Uludag provide a paradise for skiers in a climate and landscape comparable only to that of the Swiss Alps. The Celik Palace Hotel offers every possible comfort. Every room has its own bathroom, running hot and cold water, telephone and central heating. The swimming pool is very popular. Our cabaret meets the demands of the most sophisticated tastes. Orchestral music at lunch and dinner. The Celik Palace Hotel is the biggest spa hotel in the Balkans and the Near East."

Duriet listened quietly. The sound of music floated softly down from the first floor. The orchestra was playing Viennese waltzes.

"If they went on building according to my plans," I said, "the dining-room is light green and is supported on eleven columns."

We stayed in the hotel for an hour. Then we left. We did not order anything, or ask for a room.

It is an exclusive hotel. I could not afford its prices.

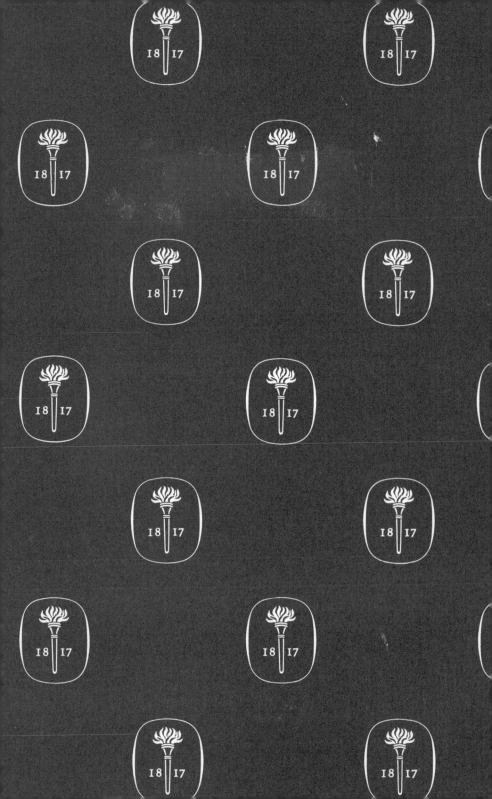